$20,000

A BOOK

by

Bill Drummond

2010

First published 2010.

Beautiful Books Limited
36-38 Glasshouse Street
London W1B 5DL

www.beautiful-books.co.uk

ISBN 9781905636846

9 8 7 6 5 4 3 2 1

A catalogue reference for this book is available from the British Library.

Cover and text design by Cally at www.antar.cc.
Typesetting by Misa Watanabe.
Printed and bound in the UK by TJ International.

$20,000

A BOOK

by

Bill Drummond

2010

Beautiful
Books

Have A Habit

21 June 2006

This is the prologue to the second edition of this book, the paperback version. The first edition was hardback, clothbound and landscape in proportion. It had 90 colour plates and the paper was of superior quality. It was an object of desire and indulgence. It was also only available in specialist art bookshops and it was published in 2002. This edition is cheaper and easier to hold, shelve and use. It has no colour plates and the paper is pulp. Three paragraphs that appeared in the hardback have been deleted as they are now irrelevant, some factual mistakes have been corrected and, as you will discover in the following pages, some of the ideas set out there I no longer hold with. It also brings this story up to date (well, to summer 2006), with 15,304 more words (never mind the quality, check the word count).

There will be a third edition. It will only be published after I have buried the money, completed the walk across Iceland, hung the picture on the wall* and this whole *How To Be An Artist* work is done with. This third edition will be a coffee-table book. There will be many more colour plates and the lost ones will be reinstated. There will be a tie-in TV documentary and a major art exhibition in a metropolitan gallery. The third edition will not be published for some years. Circumstances have a habit of changing.

*This hanging the picture on my wall may prove somewhat more difficult than planned as I no longer live in the same house.

Bury the Box and Finish the Job

This is the beginning of the text for the 2002 edition of the book.

In 1970 my sister Jane (19), and I (17) spent the summer travelling in Iceland. While there, we tried to cross the country from top to bottom. Starting at a town called Akureyri, we headed south. We only got halfway, to a volcano called Mount Askja.

The following three years, for me, were spent at art school. My ambition had been to be a painter of wild landscapes. While there I was overtaken by events and an appetite for the undoable. This led me to drop out and reject everything I had learned in art school.

Since then my life has been taken up with moving about, making careers in pop music, filling notebooks, suppressing the urge to create anything that might be mistaken for art and the usual domestic complications and celebrations.

In 1981 I became aware of the work of the Bristol-based artist, Richard Long. He made art by walking and doing things on his walks. I fell in love with his work. In the meantime, he became an internationally successful artist, winning the Turner Prize in 1989.

In 1995 I went to the Anthony d'Offay Gallery in London and bought a Richard Long photo and text work. It was called *A Smell of Sulphur in the Wind, (A Southward walk of 220 miles in 14 days across the middle of Iceland, 1994).* It was a large photo of a stone circle he had built the previous year while on a walk across Iceland, from the top to the bottom. The asking price was $20,000.

In 1998 I was asked to interview Richard Long for the Bath and Bristol listings magazine, *Venue*. I didn't. Instead I wrote a story called *A Smell of Money Underground.* It told the tale of a day trip I made to Bristol to look at a new work by Richard Long and how I was now bored with the one that I had bought, which was hanging on our bedroom wall being ignored. *A Smell of Money Underground* was published in *Venue*, the Art Magazine *Modern Painters* and my own book of stories, *45* (Little, Brown).

In April 2000 I wrote and published a pamphlet called *For Sale*. This pamphlet was for anybody who might be interested in buying from me *A Smell of Sulphur in the Wind* by Richard Long for $20,000.

The text of the pamphlet is printed below:

> FOR SALE
> Part 1
> *An idea is beginning to surface from my murky imagination. Something is evolving, maybe my relationship to the original work, or the work itself, or maybe something totally new. It's getting clearer. I will sell the photo for $20,000. Make a stout wooden box with a strong padlock. Put the $20,000 in dollar bills into the box. Return to Iceland, find the stone circle, dig a hole at its centre and bury the box. Not only will I have gone to great(ish) lengths to track down the stone circle, experienced blistered feet, aching muscles and loneliness, but if I wake at night filled with the terrors I can comfort myself with the thought of those 20,000 greenbacks in their strongbox, rotting to a worthless mush. As for Richard Long, if he ever reads these notes, will his relationship with the work change? Would that be good or bad? As he may be the only other person on earth who knows where the circle is, will he be tempted to return to the spot, retrieve the cash and put it to a worthwhile cause?*
>
> *I will take a black and white photo of the enriched stone circle, blow it up big, frame it and hang it on our bedroom wall. The title?* A Smell of Money Underground *should do.*
>
> The above text is the last two paragraphs of a story I wrote in early 1998. For the next 24 months I tried to banish the idea from my memory. When it would not be banished, I tried to convince myself I never meant it. A mere whim. Just something thrown in for effect to end the story.

Not only would the idea not let itself be banished, it kept twisting and turning in my head, forcing itself to evolve. I had visions of placards attached to safety railings at the side of inner-city expressways and suburban through-roads. Placards like those used to advertise the Bath and West show or giant car boot sales. On them I imagined the words: 'For Sale — *A Smell of Sulphur in the Wind* by Richard Long — $20,000'.

I responded to my visions by finding a printer who printed placards for estate agents. He printed me 500 red, white and black placards on a material called correx. They sat in my workroom, cluttering the place up. I was now committed to whatever it was that this was leading to.

Next, I decided to mount one of these 'For Sale' placards in a frame identical to the one in which Richard Long's work had been framed. I also planned to mount the complete version of the original story I had written, in an identical frame. Was I allowing an Art and Language retro-chic ethic to creep in?

On the back of *A Smell of Sulphur in the Wind* was a sticker giving the name and address of the picture framer used by Richard Long. It was John Jones in north London. I took one of my red, white and black placards; a blown-up version of the story; and my Richard Long original up to London and asked the man at John Jones if he could do me two frames exactly like the one I had brought with me.

'Yes sir, but would you like to have these pairs of brass screws on each of the four sides of the two new frames?'

'What are they for?'

'They serve no practical purpose, but Mr Long always insists on having them. He is most particular.'

'Then I want them as well.' If I'm going to these lengths, I may as well get really petty, I thought.

Seven days later and the job was done. I took them home and

leant the three framed pieces up against the sofa in the front room. I was very pleased with the way they looked. A faint smell of smugness was hanging in the air. A triptych, I thought to myself. And the title of the triptych would be *For Sale – A Smell of Sulphur in the Wind by Richard Long – $20,000.*

Next I left a message on Suzanne and Cale's answering machine. Suzanne and Cale are a perfect double act. Bound together by a hundred moonlight flits and a score of dawn raids. They scale social ladders and fall into gutters at the same time. I like Suzanne and Cale a lot and have done for some years. Suzanne and Cale have a habit of hosting art events; they have an aptitude for private views, gala nights and premières. Cale also has, from time to time, the added talent of inspiring people to want to punch him in the face. These people include me.

It was Suzanne, as the art editor of the Bristol listings magazine *Venue*, who invited me to interview Richard Long in late 1997.

After a few weeks of leaving messages on answerphones, we met up. I showed them the pile of 500 correx placards cluttering up my workroom and explained how I had an urge to spend a night in Bristol attaching them to railings. I then showed them my triptych and explained that for this job to be completed I would like them to exhibit the triptych in a space in Bristol. A space with no other works on show, with a big enough white wall for all three frames to be hung in a neat row. But most important of all, I wanted them to make sure that at least one of the visitors to this space would be in need of an original Richard Long and be in a position to fork out $20,000 for it.

Without that transaction, making the journey to Iceland with 20,000 dollar bills in a stout wooden box, finding the stone circle and burying the box, would all have been a waste of time, energy and money.

So where is the art? Not in the night I hope to spend fitting the placards to railings; not in the content of the three frames, even with their brass screws; not even the interesting and exciting private view and transaction of $20,000. No, the art lies in the completion of the task, in the knowledge it has been done. And of course in the satisfaction that some other bugger has *A Smell of Sulphur in the Wind* by Richard Long hanging on their wall, and is wondering what they bought.

Part 2
So I've changed my mind. It's not against the law etc, etc, etc. It's 11 days before my 'For Sale – *A Smell of Sulphur in the Wind* by Richard Long – $20,000' opens in a temporary gallery space in Bristol. Suzanne and Cale were up for the job, found a suitable location and even came up with the idea that my little show should open at 2pm on 20 May 2000; this time and date being the exact time and date that a far larger show by Richard Long opens across town at the Royal West of England Academy. I embraced their idea. But as the date has approached my feet have got cold. What seemed clever only days ago now looks like a shallow and somewhat minor stunt. What's worse a stunt done by an ex-pop star who once gained some infamy by seemingly flicking two fingers at the contemporary art establishment; whatever this whole 'For Sale' thing means to me I didn't want it reduced in this way. I would rather do it and nobody knew about it than it be seen as a shoddy bit of publicity-seeking shenanigans.

There was also another problem that I had overlooked until my son put me straight: 20 May is also the day of the English FA Cup Final. A bad day to do anything else other than win the FA Cup. I had an idea. Actually not my idea, it's a bastardisation of an alternative idea that Suzanne and Cale had.

In the next couple of weeks, on a day when the weather looks fine, I will load up the Land Rover with the 500 placards and the three framed works. Starting from the docks at Southampton I will drive up Britain, the mainland bit. From the bottom to the top. The drive will end a few days later at the Dounreay nuclear power station on that flat bit at the top of Scotland.

On the way I will stop at any railings, bits of fencing or gates I like the look of and fix one of the 'For Sale' placards. The five hundredth on the gates of Dounreay. I would like each placard to be facing east so as to greet and catch the rays of the dawning sun. This greeting and catching would go on until the last had been ripped down by whoever's job it is to rip down unauthorised advertising. Of course I will be tempted to take photographs of the placards as some sort of documentation of the job done.

If I pass any interesting cafés or other art spaces on the way I will stop, unload the three framed works and conduct an impromptu exhibition for an hour or so, hand out these pamphlets to passers-by, then pack up and get on my way to the top.

There is something else I like about this proposition. For me, this drive up Britain is also an admiring nod towards Richard Long's children's classic *A Walk Across England.*

As for selling *A Smell of Sulphur in the Wind* for $20,000. I will conduct an experiment in e-commerce. If you are interested contact shop@penkiln-burn.com. Have your credit card details ready. No time wasters please.

So that was the text from the *For Sale* pamphlet. The main body of this book deals with the story of the four days I spent driving up Britain from Southampton to Dounreay, putting up the 'For Sale' placards. As I said, the text is an exploration and celebration of our relationship with art and the landscape we find ourselves in.

Beyond the exploring, celebrating, the prime motive for producing this book is the hope that one of its readers will be inclined to shell out $20,000 (or Sterling/Euro equivalent) to buy *A Smell of Sulphur in the Wind* off me so that I can get to Iceland, bury the box and finish the job.

Crows, Rooks and Ravens
5 June 2000

'Stop!'

'Standin' in the dock at Southampton...' The Beatles are at No. 1 with 'Ballad of John and Yoko'.

5 June 1969. A lifetime later, at 10.11 am, Monday morning 5 June 2000, David Balfe and myself pulled up into the docks at Southampton. Fine, high skies, no sign of rain and little wind. I found the screwdriver, showed Dave how to puncture the holes in the correx placards and how to attach them to posts or rails using cable ties. We got to work. The job had begun. The first placard was attached to the waterfront railings. Stood back to admire it, then I took a photo to be used as evidence that the job was being done properly.

I love docks. I love ships. All that romance of the 'running away to sea' adventure thing doesn't diminish with age. Words like 'far-flung' and 'storm-tossed' never fail to work their magic on me. And as if on cue a huge freighter laden down with a mountain of containers was being hauled by a plucky tug up into the Southampton Docks to kick-start my drive up Britain.

Dave and I put a few more placards up along the waterfront then climbed back in the Land Rover. I handed Dave the *A-Z Road Atlas of Great Britain* and asked him to map read. We had to be in Bristol by 2.00 pm and pick up Chris Brook from his flat in Bath on the way.

Stacked in the back of the Land Rover were the original Richard Long work; the other two things of mine in the identical frames; a few hundred placards; a thousand cable ties; a box of tools; a sleeping bag; and my brand new carpet. In the telling of this tale, the carpet will feature from time to time. Its pivotal significance will become apparent as you turn these pages.

It, that is the carpet, measures seven feet by seven feet. It's made from pure wool; it's pillar-box red with the two words 'For Sale' cut into it using an off-white coloured carpet. I was very proud of this carpet and I couldn't wait to show it off.

Dave Balfe, friend and sometime colleague for these past 22 years, was between vocations, so I had asked him along for the ride and the conversation. Our long-term relationship has been underpinned by the occasional long-haul motorway drive when we discuss and debate all the major art and life conundrums of the day. He was only going to be with me for the first day as he was off white-water rafting down the Grand Canyon. It was a mid-life thing, he told me.

Dave is the eternal born-again atheist. His theory for the day was: 'As far as I see it, Bill, life is for enjoying.' He said it with all sincerity and I'm sure he had spent many hours thinking about life and what it's for before he arrived at this Truth. I also know he said it to spark me off as he knows that I'm a person who is fundamentally and occasionally violently opposed to enjoyment.

'Look Dave, when and if I get to my old age I don't want to look back and think, "Well at least I enjoyed myself," that just won't be good enough. I will want to know I have done my wayward duty in the great mystery of creation.'

'Bollocks Bill, you are just following your whims. This drive up Britain is just a whim. Nothing wrong with that. You have every right to follow this whim. Enjoy it for what it is and others may enjoy the fact you have done it but don't try to dress it up with mystical righteousness like you're doing your God-given duty. Like I have said before, novelty is the only thing that counts in pop music. Once the novelty of a pop performer or any other kind of artist wears off they are redundant. Never undervalue novelty.'

Dave navigated us through Southampton. I stopped a couple of times to put up placards and take my snaps. Up the M271, on to the M17, headed west then turned off and took the A36. The A36 will take us all the way to Bath. Dave had bought himself a copy of the *Daily Telegraph*. Of course, Dave is a life-long *Telegraph*-reading, Tory-voting cunt, while I'm the lifelong *Guardian*-reading, wishy-washy liberal who will flick through the tabloids just to keep in touch and occasionally buy *The Independent* to prove I'm not narrow-minded. He read me something about a new e-commerce company called burymeright.com which depressed me as it seemed to be dealing in the same area as my fledgling mydeath.net site. I managed to banish the negative thoughts by pulling up on the hard shoulder and placing a placard in among the roadside dog daisies. I love dog daisies, and always look forward to the arrival of June when these feral blooms infest many of our motorway embankments. I took a snap and felt better.

Salisbury was the first town of national note we got to. I had wanted to get to where Gainsborough must have sat and painted his portrait of the cathedral, but time and the one-way systems were not on our side. On a side street we came across a church that was now doing time as the Salisbury Art Centre. I stuck up a placard on the notice board and we got on our way.

Dave suggested we take a diversion north up the A30 so we could stick a placard on the perimeter fence of Stonehenge. When we turned west at Amesbury on the A303, I was going to tell Dave my anecdote about this being the exact spot where Jimmy Cauty and I decided to become trustees of the K Foundation. I didn't. Instead Dave launched into a Copey conversation. It being the stone circle centre of the universe, I suppose it was the best place to have a Copey conversation.

'I phoned Julian up last week.'

'How was he?'

'Good. The success of *Modern Antiquarian* seems to have mellowed him out somewhat. Knocked a few of the chips off his shoulder.'

The conversation took some twists and turns. (Oh, and if you don't know what the *Modern Antiquarian* is, its sub-title is 'A Pre-millennial odyssey through megalithic Britain' and it's a massive book that Julian Cope had worked on for over seven years and which was met with both commercial and critical success.)

'Isn't he working on an all-encompassing but vastly subjective history of rock 'n' roll?'

'No, he's working on a book about the history of the god figure. It's called *Let Me Talk to the Driver*.'

There was a lot more to the conversation all of which was eclipsed by the greatness of *Let Me Talk to the Driver* as a book title.

I fixed a placard to the perimeter fence of Stonehenge and took the snap in Julian Cope's honour. Maybe I should give him a call. We were running late. No time to stick placards on the charismatic 'Tank Crossing' signposts as we crossed the military practice zone of the Salisbury Plain.

Picked Chris Brook up from his flat in Bath. He was looking a bit rough from two weeks of over-doing it while running Club Fringe for the Bath Fringe Festival. Chris is a writer, performer, micro-storyteller but, most of all, he is a full-time smoker. He also put together the *K Foundation Burn a Million Quid* book on which, in my extremely partial opinion, he did a brilliant job.

No time to put a placard up outside the Roman Baths. Pressed numbers on the mobile phone while driving too fast.

'Is Vic there?'

'He's in a meeting.'

'Tell him Bill called and we will be about 15 minutes late.'

'OK.'

We got there 40 minutes late. Vic Ecclestone is my hero. He is everything you would want a modern cultural worker to be. He is also probably impossible to work with.

Vic was a teacher in a massive comprehensive on the Hartcliffe estate on the south side of Bristol. His mission was simple: the kids deserve non-dumbed-down arts. Whether it's a top Brooklyn hip-hop crew or the National Ballet, he gets them on the phone and tells them why they should come to the Hartcliffe estate. And they come. I wish Vic had been a teacher at my secondary modern.

I first met him after he got on the phone to Chris Brook insisting that the film *Watch the K Foundation Burn a Million Quid* should be shown at Hartcliffe comprehensive. Chris was then organising the film's selective, site-specific tour. It turned out to be one of the best days of the film's tour. In the afternoon it was the kids at the Hartcliffe comp, then down the M4 and an evening screening for the wing-collared members of the Shelley Society at Eton, as in the school Prince William went to.

Vic Ecclestone is on an extended sabbatical from the teaching trade, running a set-up called Multi A (the 'A' can stand for any positive word beginning with 'a'). His personal remit is still to bring in the practitioners of non-dumbed-down arts to work with Bristol kids who have already been dumped on by our national education system. All very patronising you may think, but Vic makes it work. In the previous few months he had got Seamus Heaney doing a workshop with the neighbourhood rap and rhymers, giving it the eternal power of poetry in the face of whatever new medium the modern world throws up. He then got Christo over from France to wrap things up. He doesn't let on to the youngsters that these people are major, important or international. Just working artists doing their job.

'Hi Bill. How's it going, Chris?'

'Vic, sorry we are late. This is Dave, an old friend.'

'Hi! Do you fancy a goat curry before you start or do you want to unload first?'

Multi A is in the heart of the St Paul's area of Bristol, the Brixton of Bristol. Dope-smokin' Rastas hangin' on the street, young black hip-hoppers looking for cars to rob to support their crack habits…or that was what clichéd paranoia told you. Dave suggested we got the Land Rover unloaded first. Maybe it had got around that we were carrying a bit of art worth $20,000.

The goat curry was good. My first audience didn't include any of the residents of St Paul's, just Parveen Akhtar and Denise Elliot who are part of the Multi A team, Paul Bartrop from BBC Bristol, Vic, Chris and Dave. I was to do my turn in the larger of the Multi A offices. We moved some chairs, shoved a desk against a wall and rolled out the carpet. Although I had a vague idea of what I wanted to impart and how I wanted to structure the event, it soon descended into an informal chat.

I kicked off by informing the six of them that I was there to try and resolve a problem. Dave was straight in with, 'You don't want to resolve any problems. You like problems. You're here to make it more problematic.'

'OK Dave, forget the problem side of things.'

'In June 1969 a man knocked on our door and told my mum that he drove to Grimsby every morning and bought fish fresh off the trawlers, then drove back down to Corby to sell the fish. There was no fresher fish to be had in Corby. Once a week he would be coming round our estate and would be happy to supply us with our fresh fish needs. In those days that was pretty much cod, haddock or plaice, all that red snapper and monkfish stuff was unheard of.

'From then on we had the freshest of fish once a week. The following June he told my mum that if any of her children wanted to go to Iceland he could organise it with one of the Icelandic trawlers he did business with. My big sister (19 at the time) thought this was a good idea and come the summer holidays my sister and I drove up to Grimsby in the back of his fish van. He was as good as his word. He got us on an Icelandic trawler. The crossing took five days...'

I then tried to give a concise version of what I had written in the story 'A Smell of Money Underground' that had appeared in the book *45* and the story 'For Sale' that was first published as a pamphlet and you have probably already read in the first chapter of this book.

'So this picture is worth $20,000. Why?' asks Parveen.

'Well...'

'It just looks like a black and white photo in a big frame,' she started again.

'It is, but...'

'How do you know it is worth $20,000, I've only got your word for it?'

'Look, I got a receipt from the Anthony d'Offay gallery that shows how much I paid for it.'

'Well that proves nothing. If I went to the supermarket and offered to pay them $20,000 for an orange and they agreed and gave me a receipt confirming that I had paid $20,000 for the orange, it doesn't mean that orange was worth $20,000. All it confirms is I was stupid enough to pay that much for an orange.' Parveen had creative opinions. This was good.

'But the orange will rot,' adds Denise.

'So will his picture in time.'

'But the orange will gain infamy as being the orange that someone paid $20,000 for.'

'Will the orange be art?'

'If the right person says it is.'

'Is the right person the girl at the checkout desk?'

'Or the man who picked the orange?'

'No, the orange decides.'

'I've eaten the orange so I decided. And what I've decided was that it was an orange worth eating and that is that.'

'I've come here to try and sell this picture, not talk about oranges.'

'But we haven't got $20,000 and even if we had we wouldn't spend it on that picture.'

'How much is it now worth, Bill?' asked Dave.

'Things are only worth whatever anyone is willing to pay for them. You know about stocks and shares, Dave.'

'But the market is maybe overvalued. So tell me, Bill, is this picture today worth more than $20,000? Yes or No?'

'Yes.'

'How much more?'

'I don't know.'

'So why don't you take it back to the Anthony d'Offay gallery and sell it back to them? Surely that would be the easiest thing to do.'

'Because I don't want to, and anyway they wouldn't buy it.'

'Why not?'

'Because when they sold it to me they would have taken 50% of what I paid them as their commission. The other 50% would have gone to the artist. If they bought it off me for, say, $23,000, they would have to resell it at considerably more to make it worth their while, which would be difficult. It is easier for them to sell new work by Richard Long than work that somebody has got bored with. What they, or any gallery, would like is to see the work of the artists they represent go for resale under the auctioneer's hammer and be sold for a considerably higher price than they originally sold it for. Then they can hike up the price of the same artist's new stuff.'

'So why don't you sell it at auction. You may get loads more money.'

'But I want to get $20,000 for it.'

'Why?'

'Because I like the sound of the figure. It's a good round amount. No pissing about. Take it or leave it. $20,000 and it's yours.'

'OK. So if one of us was to write out a cheque now for $20,000, would you take it?'

'I don't know.'

'Because you don't really want to sell it. This is all a sham.'

'No, I do. But...'

'But what?'

'But I'd want the money in cash. Twenty thousand one dollar bills. Real yankee dollars, cash money.'

'To burn?'

'No!'

'You're just making this up as you go along.'

'Well in a way, of course. This whole trip is supposed to be an exploration of an idea...'

'And?'

'And if I was to sell it to one of you right now it would make the rest of this drive up Britain redundant.

'So yes, me demanding cash money is just a stalling tactic in case you were about to whip out your cheque book, Dave.'

'This whole thing is ludicrous. You two drove here together. Why didn't you have this conversation in the car and sort all this out beforehand?' It's Parveen again.

'Because we didn't.'

'What I want to know is why you wasted that sort of money on a picture that once you got you didn't want?'

'It's just basic human nature. Haven't you ever walked past a shoe shop and seen a pair of shoes you like? And you see these shoes every day as you walk to work and you say to yourself, "I'm going to buy those shoes" and at the end of the month when your wages go in, you go out and buy those shoes and a week later you don't like them.'

'Yes, but I didn't spend $20,000 on the shoes.'

'It's only a matter of scale. It's the same thing.'

'OK. So why when you've sold the picture to whoever is daft enough to buy it, don't you give the money to something worthwhile?'

'That's not the point. The point...'

'The point is Multi A could do with $20,000. Multi A could do a lot of good with that money instead of letting it rot in a box in the middle of Iceland.'

'Yeah, I know, but that's not what I want to do. And, anyway, the money thing is only a minor part of the whole deal. I'm not doing this to make some sort of statement about art or the art market, what I'm doing is, is, is...'

'Is what?'

'Well I suppose making art, and me selling it for $20,000 is part of the making of it.'

'I don't understand this.'

'I do,' said somebody, but not me. I think it was Paul who, up until now, had been listening intently without saying anything.

'None of this changes the fact that $20,000 could do a lot of good and if you don't need it, you should...'

Dave comes in with, 'Don't you know what this man has done before? He...'

'Dave, I don't want to go into that now, that has nothing to do with this.'

'But it has. It has everything to...'

'Shut up Dave.'

'Why?'

'Because I'm asking you.'

'OK,' he says with a smirk on his face.

'To try and answer your question, haven't you got things in your house you could sell and then give the money to some worthwhile cause?'

'Yes. But. OK, I accept what you're saying. But isn't this all some sort of publicity stunt so the papers write about it: "Man sells art for less than its value and then leaves the money to rot in a box in Iceland" type thing?'

'No, and anyway this won't get that sort of publicity and even if it was going to, I would try and stop it. That sort of publicity would just kill whatever power the thing, the process, the whatever, might have, just turning it into a story in a newspaper.'

'But surely you want the papers to write about this?'

'No, because a newspaper's job is to reduce all stories about art to money, sex and "aren't they all mad?" and "isn't it all a sham?" and I'm not interested in that.'

'Publicity kills myth. Bill is trying to create myth,' said Chris breaking his sage-like silence.

'Am I?'

'Yeah, you know you are.'

'Look it's time to go. We're supposed to be in Stroud by 4.00 pm and it's a quarter to already.'

We packed up. Shook hands. Drove to Bristol Temple Meads station to drop Chris off. Stuck up a placard on one of the fancy Victorian wrought-iron lamp posts, took a picture and set off. Up the M32. North–west along the M4, on to the M5 at junction 20 and off the M5 at junction 13. These bits of motorway have no emotional hold on me, they're just stretches of tarmac to get to places. The A419 twists through Dudbridge, Stroud and on to Brimscombe, Fred West country, following the directions faxed to me by Neville Gabie.

Posts is a paperback picture book that Penguin put out in 1999. All the pictures in the book are of goal posts. Not regulation FIFA goal posts but goal posts chalked or painted on walls. Goal posts made out of branches, oil drums, demolition rubbish, anything a bunch of lads in need of a football game could use to get their game going. These pictures have been taken all over the world, from the Outer Hebrides to the beach at Ipanema, from the back streets of Liverpool to the African Bush. This book celebrates the positive side of football's globalisation. It is the extreme opposite of the "eat football, sleep football, drink Coca-Cola"-sponsored World Cup image that is used to sell anything it can. No matter how many people play cricket, rugby, baseball, grid iron or even basketball, in various parts of the world, they will never be able to touch football. All those other games require considerably more organisation to get them going. A game of football can be more easily improvised than any other sport, anywhere, any time. Anybody for a game of three and in?

Posts had been piled high on the counter of my local Waterstone's. I had a flick and instantly invested in it. On reading the blurb I discovered it was by an artist called Neville Gabie. I loved it. I bought a load of them as Christmas presents. The Bluecoat Gallery in Liverpool had put on a couple of shows around that time, one of photos taken on buses around Liverpool over the past 30-odd years, the other was of football grounds, large and small, across the British Isles. Both shows stirred my emotions in the way this book had. I phoned up Bryan Biggs at the Bluecoat to tell him of this *Posts* book and how I thought it would make the basis of a great and popular show. It turned out that Neville Gabie was then the artist in residence at the Liverpool Tate and Bryan Biggs knew all about him.

If it wasn't for Richard Long's *A Walk Across England* book and Neville Gabie's *Posts*, this book would not exist. It was *Posts* that pushed me into borrowing a camera from two of my children and taking pictures of what I did.

Gabie and I made contact a couple of months ago. I told him about my drive up Britain thing and asked if I could stop off at his place and do a show. He agreed. Dave Balfe had the fax from Gabie. He was in charge of directions. Through Brimscombe, up a leafy lane to the left until we got to a decommissioned water mill. This was Gabie's studio and home. After greetings and apologies for lateness, I unloaded the car and brought the frames into the large kitchen. The audience consisted of Gabie, his partner Joan, one of their sons, Tobias, an artist friend called David Jones, and Balfe. A pot of tea was made and I began.

I kicked off with the anecdote about the fishmonger. It felt like padding. I felt embarrassed. It felt like they were listening to my vague story out of politeness. It was only when I turned the Richard Long picture around and began talking about how I didn't notice it any longer that David Jones started to open up. He wanted a closer inspection.

'He overcooks his prints, you know that don't you?'

'Overcooks?'

'To get that grainy effect. And you can see over here on the right hand side of the print he, or whoever does his prints for him, has been up to some darkroom skulduggery.'

'What do you mean?'

'Well, someone's worked at this print to make it look meaner and moodier.'

'You mean I've been cheated? This is not a true likeness of that stone circle on the day Richard Long took the picture?'

'Of course not. It's a photograph. And a black and white photograph at that. All photography is subjective, we all know that. It's a subjective element that makes it...'

'Don't say art.'

'I was going to but...'

'Look, I have to admit this somehow undermines something I've always felt about Richard Long's work. For me there was always this Zen-like purity to it. A haiku quality. Work untouched by all the shit of the man-made world and now you are telling me about behind the scenes jiggery-pokery creating the effect.'

'I can't believe you are that naïve. Anyway, why are you doing all this? Are you trying to be a spin doctor?'

'A spin doctor? For what? For who?'

'For Richard Long. He's the last person that needs it. For over 20 years he's been one of Britain's most commercially successful artists and here you are going about the country trying to promote his work. If you have to champion someone there are plenty of better artists currently working and, anyway, for this kind of stuff Hamish Fulton is far superior.'

'But that's not what I'm doing. It's not what this is about. Richard Long's work said something to me at a certain time.'

'Yes, but since that time, whenever it was, he's done nothing new. It makes no real emotional impact. It says nothing. You walk into any big public gallery anywhere around the world, they've all got their Richard Long on the floor. You just walk around it on your way to see if they have anything interesting. They are as ubiquitous and as missable as the fire exit signs that you get in every gallery.'

'I like fire exit signs.'

'So why aren't you touring the country promoting fire exit signs?'

'Can I have another cup of tea?'

First allowing me to take a sip from my replenished cup, David Jones was off again.

'The thing about Richard Long is that he has been to all these places around the world and all he has to show for it are these few pictures of empty space where he has rearranged a few sticks or stones. I bet he has been working for years on a huge book filled with hundreds of photos, all those other pictures he took while visiting these countries. That's the book I want to see, the book that tells the real story of where he has been and what he has been up to. Not just another desert or mountain range or glacial flow but...'

I have taken the liberty of editing out what David Jones suggested this unseen work of Richard Long's might contain. This is to protect me from libel writs and Jones from embarrassment. He finished his colourful suggestions saying, 'I believe all this walks and stone circle stuff is just a front for something else and I can't wait for the real book to come out.'

'Well, that about destroys it for me. I'll never be able to look at *Circle in the Andes 1972* without thinking about the young lad he may have been buggering the night before in Lima or Bogota.'

'Good.'

Joan, who like Vic in Bristol had been the good host by not saying anything that might add friction to the proceedings, then spoke. 'Well David, I think you are wrong, I think in 100 years from now Richard Long's work will still be valid and not just as a historical footnote about English conceptualism of the early 1970s.'

'Rubbish.'

'There is something else I want to talk about. On Saturday I got a letter from Suzanne and Cale, the couple who were originally going to put this lot on as a show in Bristol. Well, they moved to London a couple of months ago and since then have embroiled themselves in some quarter of the London art scene. Have you heard of the fig 1 Gallery that Jay Jopling has set up with Mark Francis in Soho? Fifty shows in 50 weeks.'

'Yeah.'

'Well, Suzanne and Cale are regulars at the Monday openings. They would like to present a case for me showing the on-going product of whatever it is I've done, am doing now and will be doing in the next couple of days, at fig 1.'

'I can't believe you are seriously considering this. Surely Jay Jopling represents everything that you are opposed to.' It's Jones again.

'What am I opposed to?'

'The whole commodification and hyping of shallow ideas and selling the product off to advertising executives who only view art in the same way as an ad campaign with some bad-boy celeb artist providing high media profile.'

'So you don't like what he does?'

'That's not the point, I just thought everything you had done to date was violently against all that crap. If you were to go and do a poky little show at fig 1, it would undermine all the other stuff. It would confirm any suspicions people might have that you were just trying to take some short cut up the 'art-as-career' greasy pole. Do you want to pander to that London opening-hopping crowd?'

'No, but...'

'Well don't do it then. No! *Do* do it if that's what you want.'

'OK, so where do you think I should show the work?'

'In a show house on a newly built Wimpey or Bovis estate. The one with the flag outside and turf freshly down while the rest of the estate is just churned-up mud. That would make the perfect gallery for what you want.'

'Brilliant idea. I might take you up on that.'

'So what's with the 'For Sale' carpet?' asked Neville.

'I like carpets. This is the fourth one I've done. The first one was the same size, seven foot by seven foot, black with the words 'Lie Down' in the same off-white as the 'For Sale' letters. I was in this show in Sheffield and had done a big text work seven foot by seven foot. There was no room to hang it so the curator suggested I fitted it to the ceiling. I then had the idea of making the carpet with the words 'Lie Down' and positioning the carpet directly underneath the text, in the hope that people would follow my instructions and so observe the work.'

'And did they?'

‘I don’t know but I liked the carpet, I’ve got it in my living room at home. The black’s a bugger with the dogs’ hair. Has to be hoovered every day. The other two carpets were also done for exhibitions but they didn’t work so well. I got a bit too experimental with the design so I returned to the same formula: seven by seven, two words, one with three letters and the other with four.’

‘It works?’

‘When I picked it up on Saturday from the bloke who stuck it down to its backing, he told me to leave it laid out flat as long as I could to give as much time as possible for the glue to dry. So I laid it out on the ‘Lie Down’ carpet in the living room. When I came downstairs this morning and saw it there on the floor with the morning sunlight streaming through the window I was overcome by the sin of pride. It looked fantastic. A page three stunner. It only cost me just over three hundred quid to make and I reckon I could sell it for a thousand.’

‘At least,’ said Dave cynically.

‘I couldn’t stop myself from thinking, “Sod all this selling the Richard Long picture and going to Iceland, I should get into carpets.”’

‘Yeah, I’d go along with that. Stop you going up your own arse and worrying about showing at fig 1 or not.’

‘When I was in my early teens,’ said Balfe, ‘I had covered my walls in posters. Rock bands, hot rods and girls, all that stuff. Then I went to art school at 16 and started sticking up prints of famous paintings that I liked, Salvador Dalis, Warhols, Rothkos. Then this lad who was in the second year and was considered to be the coolest lad in the college told me that putting up prints of famous pictures on your wall was totally unhip. So I took them all down. Then, when I started to go to exhibitions I would buy the poster of the show. The one with the date and the place. I would then put the poster in a frame and hang that on the wall. At least then it didn’t look like you were pretending. It showed you had been to the exhibition and at least seen the real thing and not just gone down to Athena and bought a print. Then Athena started selling the exhibition posters, so that made the ones I had worthless as proof of having seen the originals. So then it had to be genuine works of art or nothing. Once I got the genuine works of art I discovered they were the wrong ones. So I went back to putting the prints of the pictures I liked in the first place up on my walls. It's easier and cheaper.'

'So what are you saying, Dave?'

'Do what feels right, whatever that is.'

Off again: twisted and turned back on to the M5 then on to the M4, and headed east into the darkening sky. Dave and I pulled up into a services to get some grub, stuck up a placard bathing in the glow of all the competing back-lit adverts.

'Bill, you know I think this is all really about money.'

'Why?'

'Because you seem to go to such lengths to deny its power over you. All you seem to be doing is...'

'What?'

'It's like you are in denial.'

'Well you're wrong. If you were to go through the work I've done in the last ten years only a very small percentage of my time and my output has been related to the might of cash. It's just that, that *very small percentage* is what people relate to, the rest of the stuff is too personal or particular for people to be aware of, let alone be interested in.'

'All the same, I think at some level you must be aware it's that part of what you do that captures peoples' imaginations.'

'No!'

'Fuck off, Bill. You know fine well it is. It's an act of gross conceit on your part to go and buy a work of art for $20,000 as a gift to yourself to celebrate the fact that you and Jimmy went and torched a million quid and now you are attempting to advertise to the world...'

'Not the world.'

'Well the world that most matters to you. To advertise, all the same, that you are now bored with the picture and not only are you going to sell it, you are going to sell it for the same price you bought it for, even though you know it's worth more. Total arrogance. I've not got a problem with that but you should admit to it.'

'No!'

'Don't just say no, what are you afraid of? "Know thyself, Bill."'

'So why *do* you think I'm selling it?'

'You said it yourself earlier today: because you don't think you're getting your money's worth from the picture. You're not getting from it the $20,000 hit that you wanted so you are doing all this so you can feel you are getting the full hit, the ultimate gram of coke up your nose all at once.'

'I don't do drugs.'

'Fuck off Bill.'

It was then that I had a flashback to a dream I may have been having as the alarm went off that morning, something about crows, rooks and ravens. I had a feeling this dream had some relevance to the proceedings of this first day in my drive up Britain. I didn't mention this to Dave. In fact, we drove on in silence. As we were approaching the M25 Dave asked if I could drop him at Heathrow tube station. Things thawed.

'Bill, how about putting one of the placards up on the nose of that giant Concord model they have on the roundabout, just before the underpass?'

'Could be good.'

We didn't. There were too many cctv cameras around and I didn't want to draw attention to myself as my tax disc had run out in January.

'Goodnight.'

'Hope you don't die on the white-water rafting thing.'

'Yeah.'

I drove home. Dave didn't die.

Can You Remember Now?

6 June 2000

This is the first question each new day asks me as the curtain is yanked back to let the darkness in. Wouldn't it be good if you could actually let darkness in? Can you remember now? I never quite manage to come up with an answer that satisfies the day in question.

This day was the next morning, Tuesday, 6 June 2000. I had to be at Muffins, Leighton Buzzard by 9.00 am. My routine was to drop off Tiger, my nearly four-year-old daughter, at her pre-school, and head for Muffins where I loaded up with caffeine, went through what I had written the day before, then hit the library to get the daily quota of words done. Muffins may have once had aspirations to tea-room status but nowadays its clientele definitely defined it as a cafe, without the accent.

However I word this, it's going to sound patronising and my generalisation will do injustice to the individual clients of Muffins between 9.00 am and 10.00 am each work-day morning. At that time of day Muffins fills up with struggling, chain-smoking, fast-ageing mothers. Some, like me, had just dropped their kids off at school; others had just finished an early shift of factory cleaning jobs; others were waiting to start their community service; others were hungover and stank of stale alcohol; others looked like they were struggling with a habit. All of them had stories to tell. All of them suspected the bloke who sat in the corner scribbling words into a black book was using these stories as the basis of some future work of fiction. I wasn't. Somebody who came with me once to Muffins told them I was a writer. It blew my cover. I liked to think they saw me as an unemployable, borderline nutcase. I never spoke to them, they never spoke to me. The odd nod and that was that.

If you ever think about Leighton Buzzard — and why should you? — you may think it's a pleasant English market town. It is, but every town, however pleasant on the surface, has its underside. I'm not going to make some Ali G-style 'mean streets of Staines' claim for Leighton Buzzard. Just don't go to Muffins if you are looking for a thatched cottage and village pond, cream tea-type experience. Muffins is owned by a Greek who never speaks and who has to run a gauntlet of jibes from the regulars every morning as he arrives clutching his bulging Tesco bags stuffed with the daily shop.

It is Pat, the manageress, a comely woman in her mid-50s who is the soul of the place. In a positive sense she is a classic matriarchal figure, the reason for the success of the cafe. I've no sooner pushed the door open than my first mug of black coffee is on my table in the corner. She has an ear for everybody's problems and never deals the dirt once they are out of the door.

I like Muffins. When I was putting the practicalities of this drive up Britain together, I fantasised about stopping off at various cafés on the way and doing my show, my sales pitch, my 'Look at me didn't I do weird.' Doing a show at Muffins was to be my trial run at a café. I had talked with Pat and the Greek the week before. Left a few of my 'For Sale' pamphlets by the till, stuck up a card: '9.15 am Tuesday 6th, Art Show for 30 mins only.' All the regulars knew it was me. I was expecting a bit of a crowd. At least the hardcore regulars.

At 9.00 am I was there setting up my stall. Pat let me push some of the tables back so I could roll out the carpet. I stacked the three framed works against the wall. Pat poured me a mug of coffee. I was well nervous. Come 9.15, other than myself, Pat and the Greek, there were only three customers: the one with 'methadone in the fridge at home', the one who was doing community service, and the one who chain-smokes but runs the local netball team.

The conversation at Muffins can vary from 'After your daffodils have flowered how long should you leave them before you cut them down? or should we tie the leaves up in a knot?' to 'How many times should you let your man beat you up before you leave him?' I couldn't recall them ever talking about art.

My partner, Sallie, our three children, Bluebell, Tiger and Flint, plus a friend of Sallie's called Christine, turned up to show support and this swelled the numbers.

'Dad, I thought this was going to be an exhibition like we went to in Belfast with music and dancing,' said a disappointed Bluebell.

At 9.23 am I got to my feet and tried to start but I didn't know how to start or where to start or why there was any point in starting anyway. The gulf between where my head was at and where these three other regulars at Muffins were at was glaring with a lifetime of different experiences, expectations and excuses. I tried with the fishmonger story but while the words were coming out of my mouth, in my head I was imagining what was going on in the heads of those three women staring back at me.

'Iceland? Who wants to walk across Iceland for a summer holiday? If you got the money, what's wrong with Florida?'

'$20,000? That would solve every problem I have in my life and he's going to shove it in a box and leave it to rot?'

'He's lying. All men lie.'

Of course these ideas of what I imagined going around their heads were just as patronising as anything that was coming out of my mouth.

I tried a different tack.

'What do you think of this picture? Forget about the $20,000. Just tell me what you think about it.'

'Well I think it's OK. I like black and white photographs. When we moved into our place there was a black and white photo in a frame in the understairs cupboard. We decided to hang it up in the living room.'

'What was it of?'

'It was of this row of skyscraper builders sitting on a girder, eating their sandwiches, hundreds of feet above the streets in New York.'

'Yeah, I know the picture.'

'Is it famous?'

'Yeah, I think so.'

'So will it be worth a lot of money?'

‘Well…’ And I tried to explain why her vastly more famous print was worth next to nothing and the overcooked print of mine was worth a load of cash. I tried to move the conversation on but within a couple of minutes one of them told me she would have to get going, her community service started at 10.00 am and she couldn’t afford to be late again.

‘I hope you sell it.’

‘Yeah, and if you do and you don’t want to go to Iceland, we’ll spend the money down the pub for you.’

‘Thanks for listening anyway,’ I said.

Kissed my children goodbye. Promised Sallie I would be back Thursday night. Rolled up the carpet. Packed up the Land Rover and headed out of Leighton Buzzard for Milton Keynes.

The night before I had pulled into a garage mechanics I use, in a village about three miles before you get to ours. Kirk’s Garage was a one-man business run by a bloke called Ray. Ray had serviced our vehicles for the last eight years. You could trust him. Ray had closed up some hours before I pulled in. I wasn’t after his diesel or professional advice. I was after his enamel-on-metal Michelin map of the British Isles, screwed to the wooden double doors of his garage. You know the ones, they always have them up beside the tyre pressure chart.

As I’d left my *A–Z Atlas of Britain* in the service station and I had long since coveted one of these enamel-on-metal maps, I climbed out the Land Rover, screwdriver in hand and removed the map from Ray’s double doors. I then popped a note of explanation through the garage letterbox. ‘Dear Ray, Nicked your map, back on Friday, will sort out recompense. Yours Bill.’ So I now had this map of our isles on the front seat to show me the way and keep me company for the rest of the drive.

I love Milton Keynes. I love new towns. I love the experiments and risks the dreaming town planners make. I love the space. I love the social engineering. I love the mistakes. I love the cycle paths and the young trees planted in rows. I love the hope and the promise. I love the future. But most all I love the fact that Milton Keynes is less than 20 miles from where we live. If I had to move and it was down to me where we moved I'd move to Milton Keynes.

'He's just saying that for effect,' Sallie might say. She might be right. But I like to think it is more to do with a nostalgia I have for the new town I spent my teen years in and a defensive streak I have for the whole genre than any attempt at irony.

I had been hoping to do one of my turns at the newly-opened Milton Keynes Gallery (MK G). I had sent some of the stuff relating to this whole process to Stephen Snoddy, the gallery director. When I phoned up to ask if he'd got it and if he was up for me doing something in the foyer for whoever had wandered into the gallery with a few minutes to spare, he was in a meeting.

So I drove up the A6147. It runs parallel to the Grand Union Canal. You'll remember from your history lessons that it was this humble strip of brown water that united our mercantile capital with the manufacturing heartlands of the Black Country and the North. Without this sluggish ditch, the industrial revolution would have been 30 years later in coming. We would have had a considerably smaller empire thus the Bosch would have won the First World War, there would have been no Second World War and you would now be able to speak German far better than you do.

Z, my sometime writing partner and bosom buddy of the dark soul, had once suggested that the pair of us get a canoe and paddle up the Grand Union from London to Leeds and beyond. He thought it could be the basis for the third and last of our *Bad Wisdom* novels. He may be right. I hope he isn't. In Z's honour I put a number of placards along the banks, lock gates and a bridge over the Grand Union. A family holiday in a narrowboat on a canal is a version of hell I have never wanted to experience.

The downside about Milton Keynes is that I am too easily drawn to it, seduced by its wide avenues and easy parking. Any excuse and I am there. I usually go there, park up and just stand and stare, wander about reading the signposts: Midsummer Boulevard; This way to the theatre and gallery district; Avebury Boulevard; This way to shopping; Silbury Boulevard; This way to Gullivers Land. It was in Milton Keynes that I first noticed that job vacancies are now always advertised as opportunities. There is always a plentiful supply of new homes. I like new homes. I wish I lived in one.

MK, as the locals call it, is liberally peppered with big municipally commissioned sculptures cast in bronze, chiselled in granite, welded in steel. Modernism where it was meant to be. Not quite Hepworth or Caro but certainly in their shadow. It is an irony-free zone. And of course there are those infamous concrete cows. Long before Tracey's bed and Damien's shark, even before Carl Andre's bricks, these concrete cows in MK dominated that space in the public's imagination reserved for the 'contemporary art is a con' category of wisdom and plain speaking. When getting the train between Liverpool and London I always enjoyed the spectacle of the static concrete Friesians as the train hurtled through MK. Sadly, that can no longer happen. Rail Track, or whoever is responsible, has allowed the bushes and trees to grow to such a height on the embankment that it blocks the view from the train.

Thousands of rail passengers viewed those cows daily thus reinforcing their iconic status on a train-by-passing-train schedule, helping to retain the place that Milton Keynes occupies in the national psyche. 'Oh yeah, Milton Keynes, that's the place with the concrete cows.' If you wanted to see those cows now you would have to track them down. You will be pleased to know that they are freshly painted black and white every year and vandals have, as yet, not taken sledge hammers to them.

Somebody once told me that Milton Keynes was built on one of the most powerful ley lines in the country. Maybe I should phone up Julian Cope, ask him if he knows anything about it. The original planners must have known all about this. They aligned the streets with those ancient Celtic sites down in Wiltshire, thus sucking up all that cosmic power to help generate creative energy in the city's enterprise zones.

Anyway, enough of the eulogy. This Tuesday morning I found

myself yet again spending too long in the city, just standing and staring at the boulevards. It's not as if I stuck that many placards up, just a couple outside the MK G and that's about it. Didn't even get to put one on the cows. It was 11.45am before I finally made it out of the place and on to the M1 at junction 14.

The Land Rover had only just got out into the flow of the traffic when a thought occurred to me – to dedicate this drive to my Mum and Dad, in the same way as authors do with their books. As you hack your way through your middle years, dealing with the responsibilities of growing children and ageing parents, you become far more aware of the struggles your own mum and dad had to go through, the compromises they had to make and what you actually learnt from them. Since my court appearance earlier in the year for covering a wall in Liverpool with the words *Dead White Man* and subsequent addition to my criminal record, I have tried to suppress any rogue urges to contaminate the virgin walls of our land with my graffiti. It wasn't working. I pulled up on to the hard shoulder under the next flyover. From the back I took the brush and can of paint, that I keep for emergencies, climbed the embankment and got to work. '*For Mum and Dad*'. Job done. The Land Rover was soon back out on the road and lost in the flow of traffic heading north. The only incriminating evidence was the paint dribbling down the inside of my right arm.

I was supposed to be in Nottingham by 12.30 for my next sales pitch. This East Midlands stretch of the M1 did not fire my imagination. I've nothing against the East Midlands, there is just no vibe factor to driving through it on the M1. That said, I pulled off and drove through the Watford Gap services to revalidate the vision I once had of Jimi Hendrix sitting there at 2.00 am drinking a cup of coffee back in 1968. Not that I actually saw him there, it was a friend's big sister. But every time that I'm in Watford Gap services I like to pretend that I did.

By 12.30 I was only passing Leicester Forest East services. I mobiled the woman in Nottingham to tell her I was running late. No rain. No hold-ups. Foot on the floor like Dean Moriarty. Crossing the mighty Trent, nodded my respect to the cooling towers belonging to various coal-fired power stations. Off at junction 25. Headed into Nottingham on the A52. Stopped to put up a placard on the 'City of

Nottingham' sign. I have no particular allegiance to Nottingham. The Clough years were golden but I was always one for Notts County, being an underdog sucker. The reason for this date, other than it being a natural stopping-off place, was Joan Howitt. Howitt was the curator of the show I was in, in Sheffield, early 1999. Since then we have kept in contact, she, by sending me late-night lucidity e-mails; me, by sending postcards from the Milton Keynes shopping centre.

Howitt lived in the Victoria Centre. The Victoria is Nottingham's massive city centre shopping mall. Every city of note now has one except Winchester which still has to put up with only having the old-fashioned kind of cathedral. Above the shopping centre were 2200 flats. Late. Late. Late. And Howitt was pissed off. She'd made a pan of vegetable Mexican chilli grub with tacos to eat it with. I was supposed to have provided the drink. Down five floors in the lift and I was in a Tesco Metro loading up a basket with Jacobs Creek. Back up, bottle opener found, carpet unrolled and I was off.

'My name is Bill Drummond. I'm here to make a sales pitch. What I want to sell you is this picture called *A Smell of Sulphur in the Wind* by Richard Long. I'm asking for $20,000. It's worth more, I will accept no less and these are the reasons why I'm selling it, etc, etc, etc ...' It went like a dream. All areas of debate were fought over, new ideas were thrown in. The hot chilli grub was good. The glass of wine was good. The view from the flat was crap. The trouble is I can't remember anything that was actually said, other than somebody suggesting they might follow me to find where I buried the box. And I told them they wouldn't be able to. My mind was beginning to blur, not because of the glass of wine or the fact that the air in his flat was heavy with dope smoke but because that's the way my mind gets when everything starts speeding up.

I struggled to find my way out of Nottingham on to the M1 at junction 26 heading north. All the way to junction 32, then it was on to the M18. The M1 had been shite. Rain, hold-ups, drizzle and tailbacks. Late. Late. Late.

The M18 was not much better. A motorway with little to say for itself. Off at junction 5 and on to the M180. Now the M180 is one of our great minor motorways. It doesn't connect any two important parts of the country. It doesn't cut through any sprawling cities. What it does is partially traverse north Lincolnshire. And Lincolnshire is in my top five counties. It's wide and open and out of the way. Whatever the weather, whichever way you are going, whatever speed you are travelling – though naturally I would recommend as fast as you can go – the skies above the M180 are always massive. The M180 is not the greatest road in Lincolnshire, that honour falls on the north-bound lane of the A15 from Market Deeping down in the fens up to Scawby in the high north of the county. The best stretch of this classic A road is that above Lincoln city. Other than a short stretch near Harton, it is as straight a road as the Romans could ever have made.

Sadly my schedule on this particular drive did not allow me to fit it in the route. I also had the conflicting desire to do as much of the journey as possible on motorway. There was always a danger in driving at speed on A roads in this country: it encouraged a sick form of nostalgia. A nostalgia for driving Aston Martins, MGs with tops down, Morgans with spoke wheels. A nostalgia for a time when there were no motorways, little traffic and no speed limits. Those were the bad times before we had huge intercontinental articulated trucks to brighten our lives.

One of the best reasons for driving on motorways is that you get to see more trucks. Now, I'm no train spotter, when it comes to trucks I wouldn't know a Scammell from a DAF and I loathe the whole concept of that Eddie Stobart-spotting malarky. What I love is the brightness and boldness and bigness of the graphics and logos on trucks.

When it was discovered in the late 1960s/early 1970s that the outside walls of truck boxes could be used to advertise the wares being hauled inside, it changed the course of art history forever. It made both American pop art and colour field painting seem small and provincial. Nothing we could see in a gallery could ever again be as big and powerful as the side of a brightly graphic-ed truck in the morning sunlight.

On a personal level I usually prefer the portrait dimensions of the back loading doors of a truck than the landscape dimensions of its side. I think it must be all the handles, hinges, lights and legal info that has to go on the truck's rear, making it all look the more tough and macho, that I am drawn to. I have an aversion to the use of photography in truck graphics. For me it has to be flat colours and bold letters and not 20-foot long tubes of Fruit Gums.

My favourite back end of a lorry then and now is a Morrison's. Morrison's is a chain of supermarkets in the north of England. When heading north it is always with a welcome anticipation that I might spot a Morrison's truck.

Of course you may be of the opinion that until something has been mediated and filtered through the mind of a validated artist then it doesn't count. I say, why wait? If something is buzzing in your brain when you hear, see or think about it, then it's doing the job, the art job. In the days when it was just beautiful sunsets or a load of daffodils, we could thank the Chief as prime artist. Things have become a little more complex than that, our landscapes are a lot more cluttered than when Wordsworth and Constable were getting filled with the awe of it all.

My vanity has to intervene here in case you mistake me for one of those people who think graphic designers — or for that matter fashion photographers or the makers of TV commercials — are artists. They are not, they are salesmen being hired to do a job.

The graphic designer's input into what is creating the buzz emanating from the back doors of a truck is pretty minimal. All sorts of other indefinable things are going off, things that I am happy to leave unknowable but all sorts of stuff to do with the modern world colliding with eternals.

At the M180's junction 5 I turned off on to the A15; eight miles north and I was up on the Humber Bridge. Of course it's a great bridge. In their own ways all bridges are mystical things but I won't waste ink enthusing about this one because I know I want to write about the Forth and Tay bridges later on. Also I was already over an hour late for my appointment at Hull Time Based Arts (HTBA) and this cut deep into my appreciation of all that the Humber Bridge had to offer.

Hull may be flat, low and mean, but it has its charms if you have time to look. I didn't. Down one-way streets the wrong way. Skidding on wet cobbles, longing for the smell of trawlers back from fishing grounds. Reversing into a tight alley, it was pissing down with rain as I unloaded.

Gillian Dyson, my contact, told me my audience had disappeared down the pub. The kettle was put on and Dyson showed me around the new HQ for HTBA. I had first visited HTBA some years ago as the guest of Mike Stubbs, the founder of the place.

In those days it was in a humbler setting with nowhere near the amount of space it has now or any of the generous quantity of IT equipment that is currently available for artists working in the space to use.

It seemed they had had a lot of help from Hull City Council. Gillian explained that in the last two or three years there had been a radical turn around in the way arts-based projects are viewed by local councils. Before, councils did everything they could to ignore their existence but now they believe that this vague thing called contemporary art can help reinvent their town's image, making it a more attractive target for international inward investors, thus improving the prosperity of the area. The councillors may not claim to have any understanding of the work that is being done but it helps when applying for grants if the proposed work is to be community-based and words like *social inclusion* and *life-long learning* are used on your application form.

A book called *Supercollector: a critique of Charles Saatchi* by Rita Hatton and John A Walker came out early in 2000. One of the main negative criticisms in the book was about Saatchi's influence over the contemporary art being produced in this country. Hatton and Walker argued that young artists were being swayed into creating work that might fit with the tastes of Saatchi and so might be bought by him, thus launching their careers. I would like to put forward the argument that his influence is minuscule compared to the combined influence of local government and those who advise how lottery funds get ladled out.

As you read this there will be hundreds of young artists filling out application forms for grants to enable them to make work. These artists will not be proposing works that they truly and purely want to make but trying to foreguess what will appeal to whoever makes the decisions about who gets the grants. You either accept that whoever pays the piper calls the tune, or you ignore any outside support and carry on creating work using whatever tools and materials you can lay your hands on.

I can't help but be an idealist about it. Make your own compromise, don't let other people inflict them on you. State sponsored art has never been worth the compromises that have to be made.

'That's easy for him to say, try telling Shostakovich.'

A mug of tea was made for me, a biscuit offered and an audience was retrieved from the pub.

One likely lad intervened my rambling monologue:

'Mr Drummond, what drives you?'

I didn't have a ready answer for him. In hindsight I wish I had said 'The Driver'. The same lad told us that while waiting down the pub for me to turn up he had fallen into conversation with a retired trawlerman and his wife.

'I tried to get them to come along and hear what you had to say but he wouldn't, he said that whatever you had to say would be irrelevant to him and his wife. So here we are, a handful of ex-KLF fans and a bunch of art students. Is what you have got to say only relevant to us?'

'I'm not here 'cause it's relevant to you or not. I'm here 'cause it's relevant to me. I'm here talking to myself, I just need some people in front of me to challenge what I say so I can hear myself better.' I didn't say that bit. I've just made it up. What I said went like this: 'The last time I was in Hull talking to people about what I do was in Hull jail. My audience then was six Category-A prisoners. They had all murdered people for monetary gain. They weren't nutters, paedophiles, terrorists, ex-KLF fans or art students. Just men who had been prevented from carrying out their trade by the long arm of the law and were now spending the rest of their lives repaying their debt to society.

'One of them said to me, "Look mate, I've got nothing against you, but you got to understand that if I'd come across you the night you and the other one did the burnin', you'd both be dead." There is a lot more I could say about that particular visit to Hull but it is irrelevant to today's proceedings.'

What I didn't tell them was I was wanting to keep the full version of this particular story for another book that I hope one day to make. The fact is I don't think I did say much that was relevant to the day's proceedings. Everything at that point seemed flat and pointless.

So I finished, packed up and got out of Hull and on to the most alluring, powerful, even magical motorway on our lump of an island. Even saying its name fills me with a longing. The M62. The greatest motorway ever made. Chuck Berry can keep his Route 66, Kerouac his two-lane black top, Paul Simon his New Jersey Turnpike, Billy Bragg his A13. Give me the M62. Driving it east to west is always best, especially at the close of the day into the setting sun. I won't give a junction by junction account of why I think the M62 is so inspiring. Partly because I can't be bothered and partly because I don't know but mostly because I want to tell you something else.

As I kept my foot on the floor chasing the end of the day across this sacred isle I was wracked with guilt regarding the undiminishing pile of 'For Sale' placards in the back of the Land Rover. Since entering Nottingham I had not stopped to put one placard up. Not one under the vast skies of the M180. Not one on the Humber Bridge to celebrate all the fowls that make the tidal flats of the Humber their home from home. Not one by where the remains of the once mighty trawler fleet brought back King Cod for the chip shops of the land. And not one at the ten places or more along the verges of the M62 that screamed out for one of these placards to anoint its greatness.

It seemed to me as I rushed and roared across the flat lands of the East Riding that the whole point of this drive up Britain was to put up these placards. The stopping-off chat bits were only sideshows. And there I was ditching the main event just to placate my secondary guilt about getting to the next appointment with a 'handful of ex-KLF fans and a bunch of art students' in time. A notion had crept in and tempted me. I could cheat. I could save some of the placards, come back at a later date, put the placards up and take photographs of them at my leisure. Nobody would be any the wiser. I could still put them in this book as if I had got the lot up in one four-day rush of conflicting emotions. I suppressed the guilt as I'm able to do with so many of my emotions.

So on past the rugby league towns of Castleford, Featherstone, Wakefield, Leeds, Bradford, Huddersfield and Halifax. Up and over the high Pennines and careered down across the top of Greater Manchester. Skidded down on to the Lancashire plain. Past Warrington, Widnes and Saint Helens.

Out the corner of my eye I saw a signpost for Wigan and I thought about the Casino and three questions presented themselves. Is Major Lance still out there on a tour of one-night stands? Who needs northern soul these days? Is there anyone left to keep the faith? A few miles more.

Brakes screeched, the M62 came to a halt all too soon in a heap of a hump at Knotty Ash. And then it was under the ring road flyover and into Liverpool proper.

Liverpool is loaded with too many emotive memories, issues and sores still open to a rubbing so I won't go into them. Past the shuttered shops and kicked-in bus shelters. Down the streets I know too well. Down past the uni and the Everyman. Turn right at the Phil and down. Turn left at the burnt out church into Berry Street, left again into Roscoe Lane. Mind rushing, buzzing, speeding.

Hand brake, foot brake and clutch all together. Leapt out. Round to the back of the Land Rover, flung open the door. Pulled out the roll of carpet. In through the back of the Hub Café. Through the kitchen. Candle-lit tables, chattering people. And on to the floor. I felt like a master showman, confident that all my tricks would work. Rabbit from hat. Doves from hanky. Cards from palm of hand.

'Excuse me sir, can I move this table a few inches. I have a carpet I need to roll out.'

And out it rolled. An audience captivated by the wonder of my rug. A couple of trips out the back and I'd got all my props and I was off.

'Good evening. My name is Bill Drummond and I'm here to make a sales pitch. What I'm selling is...' My anecdotes were now well-oiled. I knew which ones worked and in which order. I knew when to slip in the self-deprecating aside, when to throw questions back at the audience.

And the carpet? Suddenly and instinctively I knew what the carpet was for. It was my space. The boxer has his ring; the golfer his green; the batsman his crease; the player his stage; but I had my carpet, my magic carpet. And I was king of my carpet. Nobody dared step on it. Thrones? Who needed them?

And when it was over I left them wanting more.

Off into the night. Well, over to the kebab shop across the road for a dripping and greasy king-size kebab and can of Coke and then off into the night.

Back up the Liverpool streets I had come down less than two hours previously. I stopped off a couple of times to stick up placards. The plan was to make the border by midnight.

Back on to the M62. No magic this time. Then at junction 10 I turned north on to the M6. I hate this stretch of the M6. I was knackered. Spent. Needed a place to rest my head. I had my sleeping bag and a fantasy that any barn would do. Somewhere in a hay loft in the *auld country* seemed like a dream too far.

I got as far as the Burton-in-Kendal services. Slunk into the Travel Lodge, got myself a room. Fell into the bed fully dressed. Lights out. Drained, but sleep didn't come, in my head wild beasts still charged across unfenced plains.

The reality was the Liverpool event had not gone as well as I've documented above but, compared to Hull, it was supreme. Some background. The Hub Café is an offshoot to a cycle shop. The place is run by Simon O'Brien who happens to be the son of a friend of my ex-wife but that's not the reason why the venue was chosen. The reason was that I had phoned up Bryan Biggs at the Bluecoat Gallery. Biggs had been in my year at art school back in 1972. He was now a senior player and inspirational figure in the visual arts across Merseyside. I had asked Biggs to recommend a place where I could make my sales pitch in Liverpool. He recommended The Hub. I'm glad I heeded his recommendation.

But the main thing that was keeping the wild beasts charging around my head and stopping sleep from rescuing my body was an unanswered question, a woman at The Hub had asked, 'Mr Drummond, are you trying to be an artist?' Whatever answer I had given her may have sufficed at the time and allowed me to move on to whatever anecdote I was to spin next. But in my Travel Lodge room, the question kept coming back again and again and again. And no answer I came up with seemed to quench the question.

Back in 1973, I had dropped out of art school. I had had my reasons, good reasons that I may deal with elsewhere. I was running away, running anywhere and everywhere. Running away to sea. Not to seek fame and fortune, though it seems they found me. So I ran away again. Always trying to find the wilderness. But the wilderness seemed to be allusive. At my heels there was always this snappy dog. It yaps many things, one of which is 'Art school drop out. Art school drop out. You failed. You failed.'

It didn't matter how much I kicked it and how much I ran, I still found myself coming back again and again and again to the same question that dogged me as a student in 1973. I'd spent my adult life doing everything I could not to be an artist and avoiding all the monomaniacal bollocks that comes with it. Every day I tried to come up with some justification to prove what I did was not art. But it was getting harder and I couldn't run so fast anymore.

'No Miss, I've done everything I can not to be an artist but it seems, from the very fact that you ask the question, I'm obviously failing.' It was not the answer I gave her in The Hub and it may not have been a wholly honest answer to give but it is the answer I would have liked to have given.

Sleep did come.

I would like to interrupt the flow of this story by telling you something that has just happened to me. Right now I'm sitting in the coffee shop of Aylesbury's Safeways Supermarket. If you have read 'My Modern Life', a story in the book *45*, you will know this is where I come at the beginning of most working days to have my first coffee and attempt to correct what I wrote the day before. One of the staff was clearing and wiping the tables. She got to my table and said, 'You do a lot of homework here. What are you studying for?'

'It's not homework. I write books and I come in here every weekday morning to go through what I wrote the day before.'

In the past it would have been my instinct to lie about what I do, cover my tracks, but I'm trying to get in to an honesty trip.

'You write books, ones that get published?'

'Yeah.'

'There was a boy who used to work here but he went to university. He came back to visit a couple of weeks back. There was a book he had to read as part of his course. In the book was a description of this café and a description of him and a description of somebody that had to be me. It wasn't you that wrote the book, was it?'

'Well, I don't know,' I lied.

'It had a big *45* on the cover.'

'Did it?' I had a sickly, uncomfortable smile on my face. A smile that needed wiping off.

'Well maybe I'm adding two and two and getting five.'

'Maybe.'

She moved on to clear and wipe other tables and I went for a wallow in my guilt. Yes it was me and yes it was her. And the description of her wasn't flattering. It went something like this — 'One young woman is very short and wears thick round specs.' That was it. Oh, why hadn't I said she has a lovely smile or a great arse? Both true but that's all too late now.

'What a fuckin' creep.'

My Life as a Trawlerman

7 June 2000

Next morning I stopped for breakfast at Killington Lake services, where I left my mobile in the bogs and have been mobile-free ever since. Two mugs of coffee and I headed back out on to the M6. This is one of my favourite stretches of the M6. From Killington Lake to junction 40, the Penrith turn-off, is classic. There's a twist in the motorway, Langdale Fell on the east side and Whinfell Beacon on the west, where you can make something happen. For it to happen you have to be driving north. I had tried various times while driving south. It never worked. You need a bunch of articulated trucks in the middle lane, in front of you. You then have to pull out into the outside lane in an attempt to overtake them, knowing that there is a car already coming up in the fast lane and you are going to seriously piss its driver off by pulling out. As you are overtaking the first of the lorries and the driver behind you is still flashing his head lamps in a fit of suppressed road rage, take more than a glance over to Langdale Fell. High in the fells you will see a dry stone wall stretching over the hump of the summit and out of sight. Dry stone walls being one of the few justifications for any celebration of the past. There are days when I know dry stone walls are our island's greatest gift to civilisation. To have built that wall over Langdale Fell is as Zen as a craft can get.

Now what you have to do is gaze as long as you can at that wall, with your foot on the floor, without letting your eyes drift back to the reality of the road in front of you. And if it's going to happen, it will happen then. That's it. It is as if all of the past that ever had existed and all the future that ever will exist, collide into each other, to create a now more pure than anything you have experienced before. Epiphany in the fast lane. Fuck sex or giving birth or going to war or all those other minor experiences like painting the Sistine Chapel or being James Brown, this is, for these few seconds, what makes life worth the waiting for.

I pulled up and fixed a placard to a signpost in honour of the waiting. Got back and drove to Scotland feeling nothing could stop the universe now.

I would advise that it is always best to drive alone. Driving with someone else might be good company but always seems to nail your mind down to reality. Rationality has a tendency to hang around like a bad smell. Is driving alone with a spurious destination better than going to the Tate Modern?

Answers on a postcard to someone you haven't seen for five years.

The M6 evolves into the A74 and the A74 becomes the M74 but it's all the same road and if you're not having to stop to put up placards you would never have to shift out of top gear.

Out over the north Cumbrian flatlands, Carlisle to the west and somewhere else in the east. Over the Esk, the sunlight glinting on the Solway Firth, then over the Sark into Scotland. Stopping at any excuse to put up my placards. Through the Southern Uplands, trying to quell whatever vestiges of nationalism I may have left in my bones. Every ex-pat of whatever nationality suffers from bouts of cheap romanticism when thinking of home. I'm probably worse than most. I'll try to keep it under control.

There was bags of time to savour every stop I made knowing that in the next 30 minutes I was going to witness one of the major hits of this drive up Britain. And there it was, and there it will be again as I write up these notes. The industrial heartland of the West of Scotland stretched out before me. Hamilton, Motherwell, Coatbridge, bathed in sunlight like a Blakean vision of a new Jerusalem. Glasgow, where kids will be worrying how pure their heroin is, fathers will be worrying about how long they can stay on or off the brew, mothers will be worrying about their tits and if they will sag in the way their mothers' did. And the Park Head faithful will be worrying if Martin O'Neil can bring back the Jock Stein years and the Ibrox Hun worrying he just might while Partick Thistle will be thinking 'Fuck the lot of you.'

Of course, I'm getting too parochial even for those living out in

Bearsden, let alone you. But you have to understand I was feeling like Dean Moriarty and Sal Paradise rolled into one having just driven across every state in the union and now gunning down into Frisco. Does that explain why I was getting parochial? I don't think so.

High-rise tenement blocks. Desperate leaps of regeneration. Screaming 'miles better' with the G and the O, done in bold. GlasGOw, that big, bad and banging city where I saw my first pantomime, *Sinbad the Sailor*. I wasn't yet five but these things stay with you. If Sinbad could sail those seven seas, then come home and tell his tales of one-eyed cannibal giants, why not me?

Off at junction 4, on to the M73 for a couple of miles then on to the M8. The M8 is not epic like the M6 or the M62 and doesn't have the big skies of the M180.

But what the west coast stretch of the M8 has, that no other motorway in this island does, is that it cuts right through the heart of a major city. From the M8 you can see all the insides of Glasgow turned out. You can see why it is 'miles better' and all the other hyperbolic shite angling for inward investment. What you don't see is why it has more alcoholics per head of the population than any other Western European city, a fact I have just made up on account of me having a poetic licence, officer.

Sadly, I had to pull off the M8 at junction 15 before I had a chance to take in all the motorway had to offer. Down past Saint Mungo's Cathedral and I got lost in the city centre, stuck in a one-way grid system of red sandstone and Victorian enterprise. I tried to get my bearings from street names chiselled deep into the part of my brain where nostalgia thrives. Charles Rennie Mackintosh gazed down from the art school and gave me a knowing sneer as if to say, 'There goes another one.' I shout back, 'Gaudi was better,' a fact I don't believe but I couldn't take the past having a go at me lying down.

I was supposed to be at my destination — a tower block up in Townhead — by noon and I would have been if I hadn't been stuck behind a posse of fire engines trying to put a fire out by the hotel in George Square where my school mate Peter McMahon had had his wedding do in 1975.

My host was Keith Farquhar. I had never met Farquhar before but we had spoken numerous times on the phone. He had first contacted me a couple of months earlier. He had been interested in me contributing a neon Tennants' 'T' for a show that he and fellow artist, Lucy McKenzie, were putting together called 'Neilsen's London', the Nielsen being Dennis Nielsen the mass murderer of teenage boys. I had designed this large neon Tennants' 'T' for a play called 'Cruel Britannia' by Johny Brown, but it was now providing illumination in a London pub called The Foundry. 'Nielsen's London' was to be a celebration of the culture of Scots from the industrial belt getting seduced by the road south to London, then finding themselves stuck there in a destructive cycle of whichever destructive cycle they found the most seductive. The neon Tennants' 'T', which they had seen in The Foundry, seemed in their eyes to be an emblem of this condition.

This 'Nielsen's London' exhibition had not happened yet, it might never happen. I hoped it would. But me stopping off at Keith Farquhar's flat did. The flat he shared with Elizabeth Harris was on the ninety-eighth floor or at least that was how it felt when you stared out of his kitchen window westward across Glasgow to the Erskine Bridge and beyond. Farquhar's front room was packed. We made a dash to the offie to get a generous carry-out. Farquhar had prepared genteel nibbles. The guests were a cross section of artists currently working the rich alluvial belt of the central lowlands. Some had made the train trip over from the east coast. I was made to feel welcome.

And I began. It was a tumbling and rumbling sort of show. No show biz, no posing on the 'For Sale' carpet, just shouting and laughter, taking the talking this way and that, pulling ideas apart, then throwing them out the window just to watch them fall and wonder at the pattern they made below as they hit the ground 113 floors down. All the Jay Jopling, Anthony d'Offay stuff. They were a worldly bunch but not worn down by reality. Still had the eagerness of the innocent. Still had marks to make and knew they deserved to make them. Sweeping generalisations of course, I was in their company for less than 90 minutes. They could have been a bunch of bitter, cynical cunts after I left but I didn't think so.

Andy Anderson aka Dr Nuepop, who was older than me said more than everybody else put together and everything he said was worth the saying, not least for the conviction with which he said it. An open invitation had been given, by one of the guests, for me to stay with their father in Orkney.

'He's a grand man and would love to hear your tale. Why stop at Dounreay? Carry on up Orkney, then over to the Fair Isle, then up the Shetlands. From there you could get a trawler to the Faeroes by which time you're near enough to hop across to Iceland.'

Chad McCail said, 'Doesn't it concern you that all you may be doing is inflating the value of the original Richard Long work for whoever buys it off you for $20,000?'

'I don't think so.'

'Well then, does it concern you that you might be making art about art?' asks a man with a hat.

'Is that wrong?'

'It is a bit of an unwritten golden rule not to do so. It's considered the ultimate self indulgent act an artist can commit. It means art just goes round in circles. It speaks to no one else other than those involved in the art process.'

'I'm sure you're right.'

'But does it worry you?'

'I don't think so.'

'That's the same answer you gave Chad.'

'Sorry.'

Dr Neupop had compromising stories to tell about Anthony d'Offay's youth in Edinburgh. And I asked a question: 'If it wasn't about money, what would you rather have *A Smell of Sulphur in the Wind* or the 'For Sale' carpet?'

'The carpet,' came the answer in a rough form of unison. And I was pleased and this is what I said, 'Well, if it wasn't for our host, Keith, this carpet wouldn't exist. We were talking on the phone a couple of weeks ago and we were discussing where we should have this get together. The original idea had been a studio or a makeshift gallery but when I learned he lived in a council flat in the tallest tower block in Glasgow with an epic view I asked if we could have it here and he said, "Fine, it can be a carpet-style show. There should be more carpets in galleries and less white walls." I agreed, of course. Who wouldn't? Not only did I agree, that remark of his got my mind working. As you can probably tell I'm into carpets. I had already done three why not a fourth? The next day I went ahead and got this one in motion. The way it is looking now this carpet may be the most positive thing to come out of this whole job.'

Somebody had to leave for their Restart appointment.

Dr Neupop was of the opinion that my carpet was the missing link between Warhol's cow wallpaper and *The Thoughts of Chairman Mao*. I wanted to agree with him but didn't know how.

'For Sale' placards were handed out to all the guests with a request they display them wherever they saw fit. I also handed round a placard and asked them all to sign their names on the back, something I wish I had thought of doing at each stop on the way.

'I'd better get going, I'm supposed to be in Dundee by 4.00 pm.'

'Where abouts?'

'Generator.'

'Oh yeah, that's a good place to be doing.'

'Before you head off we should go down to the Buchanan bus station to put up some of your placards. It's where the buses arrive from and leave for London.'

So a bunch of us trooped down to the bus station to put up placards. I felt very self-conscious, doing my business as the honest citizens of Glasgow waited with bulging shopping bags for buses to Maghill and Riddrie.

Time to pack up and wave goodbye. Chad McCail gave me an envelope. It was only when I opened it later that I realised he was responsible for the strip cartoon of the Garden of Eden story as featured in the Becks' *Futures* Show at the ICA. It was my favourite at the show even though I understood why the art media went for the Lucy McKenzie Olympic painting.

So back up on to the M8, I was trying to get out of Glasgow. With all this renaissance of Scottish art stuff going on it was hardly surprising I was overtaken by the fantasy that I would see Douglas Gordon hitchhiking, holding his placard with the word 'psychopath' felt-tipped on to it. I would have stopped to pick him up on the understanding that he didn't kill me until he had at least navigated me out of Glasgow and out on to the A8 heading east.

There was no Douglas Gordon and the A8 and the eastern portion of the M8 are so boring I decided to see how much of Douglas Gordon's *24-hour Psycho* I could replay in my head. What I found myself doing was slowing it down even further. It was now Bill Drummond's *100-hour Psycho* and there were no bean bags to lounge on and watch it, just the dismal West Lothian landscape to try and ignore. Is this what the West Lothian question is all about?

As I think I've already mentioned, the camera I was using was on loan from two of my older children, Kate and James. It was an Olympus Newpic Zoom 600. It's ridiculously easy to use. Automatic focus and light meter, just point and press. The same with loading and unloading it, you just flick a switch and drop in a cartridge. You never actually see any film or negatives or anything. Just take the cartridge into Boots, go back the next day and get your pictures. You've probably got one, so I don't know why I'm telling you. It hypes all the colours up. Turns even the mildest blue skies into screaming azure. Yellow it can't cope with and makes black anything but. I like it this way. Takes any responsibility for what the pictures look like out of my hands. All becomes subject matter, well almost. Obviously I must like this trashy holiday snap vibe. As for blowing them up, not worth it, Boots can only blow them up twice the size but they look shit.

Since learning the basics of photography on art foundation course in 1970, I have not picked up a camera since. Other people took pictures, not me. But on this drive up Britain I found myself beginning to take pictures that were nothing to do with the placards. I was taking close-ups of bits of the outside and inside of the Landrover that I liked the look of. Did this mean I was beginning to fetishise the vehicle? Probably, best just accept it as a necessary weakness. I mean why else take a picture of a diesel cap or a gear stick?

Now for the sake of speed I should have taken the A80/M80/M9/A9 route but that would have meant missing out on crossing the Forth Road bridge. No drive up Britain would be worth the pollution generated by your journey if you did not cross the Forth Road bridge.

So it is off the M8 at junction 2, head north for a couple of miles on the M9, then off at junction 1A and across to the A90.

Toll paid and I was up on to the bridge. This is the second greatest bridge in the land. What makes it almost better than the greatest is the parallel view you get of the greatest bridge in this land while crossing it.

If this sounds confusing, it's because it is. The greatest bridge in this land is the original rail Forth Bridge. The one they are always painting. Now there is a job for a fledgling painter with an MA still fresh in their hand: spend the year painting the Forth Bridge, then go and stand on the road bridge, take a photo of the epic scale of your handiwork with brush and paint, blow it up huge, take the big picture down to London and impress the people.

My Granny Drummond, who was born in the early 1880s, was fond of telling me about the time when she was a small girl and she was going to be taken for a train ride over the newly-opened Forth Bridge for a treat. But as the train pulled out of Dalmeny station and she could see from the carriage window the huge leviathan monster of a beast they were going to have to do battle with, she started to scream. Nothing before in the history of mankind had been so big and epic. The Hanging Gardens of Babylon mere myth, the pyramids just a pile of rubble, Stonehenge just a tourist attraction.

No, the Forth Bridge was the most epic construction the Victorian world had ever seen and in the eyes of my granny it must have looked like it spanned an ocean. Her initial fear had been inspired by the idea that the train had to go over the humps. When it was explained to her that this was not the case, that the train would be driving through it, her fear got more extreme. She believed that as they approached the bridge the train and all its occupants were going to be eaten whole by the humpbacked monster. Into the belly of the beast they would go. She loved to tell the tale of how she survived and they had afternoon tea at North Queen's Ferry to celebrate before heading back home.

There was no time for me to stop and wonder at the glory of either road or rail bridge, just a quick glance east to see if I could see Inchkeith Lighthouse out in the spreading Firth of Forth. I could.

And down into Fife and on to the M90 heading north to Perth. This motorway holds little charm. The only things that can be said for it are that it heads due north and it passes Loch Leven. My interest in Loch Leven had nothing to do with the way it looks. It might be the most boring looking loch in all of Scotland. Nothing dark and scary like its namesake sealock on the West Coast. I'm also not interested in the admittedly rich history of its two main islands. No, my interest lies in that it is the only place in the world that is home to a variety of powan.

'What the fuck is a powan?'

'And who the fuck cares?' ask a pair of readers in Reading.

A powan is a fish and I care. I will resist spending the rest of this book talking about the mythical status that the lives led by each variety of fish to be found in these islands have in my head. It is enough for you to know that the powan is a lesser known member of the coregonus family of fish and a distant relative of the salmon. I may be in danger of sounding xenophobic in what I say next. If I am I will seek a cure. Powan are found in a select few of our lakes and lochs. It is not some exotic interloper that arrived here like the North American crayfish or the grey squirrel polluting our land. It is a native. Been here since the last ice age retreated. That's as native as you can get. And it's wild, never knowingly to be found on the menu of even the most avant-garde of London fish restaurants. And in Loch Leven is a variety of powan not to be found anywhere else. Now I like evolution and only wish it happened fast enough for me to see the feathers of the sparrows on our bird table change colour as I watch.

The thing is, if Darwin had known about the powan he need never have spent all those months bored on the Beagle and years running around the Galapagos Islands chasing finches. He could have learnt all he needed to know from checking the varieties of powan that exist in our lakes and lochs. Each of these sub-species have been cut off from the other since the last big melt and have thus evolved their own idiosyncrasies to deal with life in their own stretch of land-locked pond.

So between junctions 5 and 6 of the M90 cast your gaze east and take in the view of Loch Leven. Your reward will not be big and epic. It is a lot more subtle than that but it is a kinda wonder all the same. There, on my drive up Britain under a rather dull sky was the surface of a rather dull water. But under that dull water was the entire population of a fish, quietly evolving into its own distinct species.

Of course I know that any and all life forms that we see in our daily lives are doing the same but I always use those few spare minutes between junctions 5 and 6 on the M90 to marvel at nature's hidden ways and pay homage to this particular brand of the powan's journey towards extinction. Or the stars.

I've taken a break from making these notes to check some of my facts about the powan in my collection of books on fish. Devastated would be too strong a word, more confused. There was no mention along the entire length of my shelf of books on British fish, that the powan has ever existed in Loch Leven. For 30-odd years I had been passing Loch Leven, marvelling and paying homage, only to be confronted with the fact that it was all in vain.

This is an example of why I distrust the past: it plays tricks on you, evolves untruths, meddles with the future, undermines the present.

The next time I return to my fish bookshelf I might find no mention of the powan at all, in any lake, loch or garden pond. Maybe the future extinction of all species of life on this planet will have nothing to do with global warming or over-fishing but a bit-by-bit disappearance from the records leaving just the myth behind. Was this what happened to the dragons and mermaids? Will the Loch Leven powan become a mythical beast in my head alone?

Time to change the subject. The weather? No story about driving up Britain should exist without a few passing comments on the weather, supposedly the national obsession. The weather was pretty nondescript, nothing extreme, no blistering heat, no torrential rain, just overcast. Grey, with the odd ray breaking through to dapple the landscape. No sunlight to send Vincent mad, nothing to make Hockney leave LA and come back home. Just a grey day. I like grey days, you know where you are with a grey day.

So, it was up and over the Ochil Hills and down towards Perth, home to Saint Johnstone FC and the ancient seat of the Drummond clan but I didn't stop. Bypassed the town and on to the A90 heading east–north–east for Dundee. Just after I passed Kinfauns Castle but before I got into the Carse of Gowrie stretch of road I got into thinking about the Stone of Scone. No Scottish education is complete without learning about the Stone of Scone or the Stone of Destiny as it is also known. Scottish history is forever entwined with this lump of rock. The reason for slipping into these thoughts was that I had just passed the turning for Scone where the stone has spent much of the last 1000 years. What got to me, more than any of all that patriotic stuff about the stone, was that it was this lump of rock that the Bible says Jacob used as a pillow the night he dreamt about the ladder with the angels.

When, as a kid, I first saw the stone under the throne in Westminster Abbey I thought, 'Why the fuck did Jacob choose such a huge lump of rock for a pillow? Surely he could have just made himself a mound of sand, being in the desert, that would have been far more comfortable?' This question has never been answered.

And seeing as I've just been confronted with the disappearance from all records of the Loch Leven powan I have a suspicion that if I was to check in Genesis, chapter 28, verse 18, it would no longer read: 'And Jacob rose up early in the morning and took the stone he had put for his pillows, and set it up for a pillar, and poured oil upon the top of it.

And then stuck a stamp on it and posted it off to Caledonia with strict instructions about all the kings of God's own country henceforth being crowned on it.'

While I'm on the subject of Genesis, chapter 28, I would like to take this opportunity to announce that this chapter contains the most dangerous words ever written. These are the words:

> And he dreamed, and behold a ladder set up on the earth, and the top of it reached to heaven: and behold the angels of God ascending and descending on it.
>
> And, behold the Lord stood above it, and said, I am the Lord God of Abraham thy father, and the God of Isaac: the land whereon thou liest, to thee will I give it, and to thy seed;

> And thy seed shall be as the dust of the earth, and thou shalt spread abroad to the west, and to the east, and to the north, and to the south: and in thee and in thy seed shall all the families of the earth be blessed.
>
> And, behold, I am with thee, and will keep thee in all places whither thou goest, and will bring thee again into this land; for I will not leave thee, until I have done that which I have spoken to thee of.

If only Jacob had not dreamt of that sodding ladder but had dreamt of some olive thighs belonging to the daughters of Canaan, the history of mankind would have been totally different. None of that promised land stuff, no Moorish invasions, no Crusades, no International Zionist Conspiracy, no Holocaust, none of all that Palestinian/Israeli trouble that is always threatening.

Four short verses, and mankind has been fighting it out ever since. Nothing comes close; even God's original promise to Abraham doesn't carry the weight these words do.

Right now, as you are reading this, somebody is loading a Kalashnikov or an M16 in readiness to kill somebody else as a direct result of those words having been written. This isn't me making up stuff for effect like my misremembered verse about Jacob posting the stone off to Caledonia, this handful of words can decide the fate of mankind.The section of the A90 along the course of Gowrie is a dull stretch of road. All you need know on the practical front is that more raspberries, my favourite summer fruit, grow in these passing fields than in the rest of the world combined, although I fear that the bulk of this crop was destined for the over-sweetened, mass-produced jams that Dundee is famous for. It was dull bits of information like this that inspired my mind to think about how the Old Testament postal service ever got the Stone of Destiny up the Firth of Tay in the first place.

As I stopped to fit a placard to the Welcome to Dundee sign, I knew I had to crash-land my mind into reality and find the way through Dundee to my pre-arranged destination and whoever might be there to watch me unroll the carpet.

The grey day had shifted. Afternoon sunlight was spilling gold on to the hi-tech industrial estate as I took the A85 shore road into town. The Tower of Pisa leans, the spire in Chesterfield twists and the bridge over the Tay bends. I turned left where the Tay Bridge bent into the bank. Up into the old town, home to the Broons, Oor Wullie and Generator.

But first some background. On 1 May, I was putting up a mydeath.net presentation in Belfast. I had the run of a vacant shop in the North Street Arcade in the city centre. I was trying to hang the frames and making heavy weather of it when in walked this lad with a heavy Belfast accent, specs and a helping hand. The helping hand came in useful 'cause as we spent the next couple of hours chatting about how contemporary art can flourish away from obvious hot-house zones, he gave me invaluable help in hanging the presentation. I learnt his name was Jonny Hanna and he was home for a few days visiting his folks. He was living in Dundee where he had done a degree in Fine Art. Instead of getting the bus down to Hoxton Square and pitting himself against the hordes, he decided to stay on in Dundee and see what could be done there. Inspired by the Catalyst Centre in his home town of Belfast, he had helped set up Generator.

Generator is an artist-run organisation. It exists to encourage young artists in Dundee to show their work locally and interact in whatever way possible with the people of the city. They also host visiting shows by artists from far afield or just down the road. They have a space on the Mid-Wynd industrial estate near the city centre. That was my destination. After the usual problems with one-way streets and 'no entry' signs, I rolled up so late that any form of apology was worthless. To make matters worse there was no bar, light refreshments or even a kettle and tea bags for them to fill in the wait with. While I had been ruminating on the powan and the quality of Jacob's choice of pillow, a bunch of folk had organised their day so they could spend an hour in the afternoon listening to me, give my 'Yes, the reason why I climbed Mount Everest as a statement against altitudenism was...' – type bollocks.

There were 20-odd young artist types lolling around in the sunshine looking listless. The guilt factor made it difficult for me to look any of them in the eye. Jonny Hanna was there and he gave me a hand unloading my bits from the Land Rover and carted them into the light industrial unit that was the current home to the Generator project.

There was plenty of space but no chairs and no natural light. So it was a leaning on walls or squatting on the bare concrete floor kind of show. I went through my patter and struggled to get any sort of interaction going. They were a younger crowd than at Keith Farquhar's flat. A more waiting-to-see crowd. Not verbally challenging but there was a vibe that later that evening, back in their flats, they would be giving it, 'Well, that was a waste of time' and, 'Total indulgence!' I tried to provoke debate but found it hard going. I did remember to ask them all to sign their names on the back of one of the placards. This they consented to do.

As I was packing up I was approached by a member of the audience. He introduced himself as Norman Shaw. He was from the Hebrides, not the new ones in the Pacific but the old ones off the west coast of Scotland. He was in Dundee doing a PhD, something to do with the myth of the Highlands in modern culture. He had a strange proposition. British Nuclear Fuels had offered a substantial amount of cash for him to put together an art performance/show/project at Dounreay Power Station.

'What! In the power station itself?'

'Yes. In the dome. You know, the big golf ball.'

'But surely that's the heart of the matter, the most dangerous bit.'

'Seems not. According to them it has been completely decommissioned, swept clean of any crumbs of radiation and is ready to be turned into a willing venue for contemporary art. I was about to dismiss it out of hand but when I heard that Dounreay was your destination, I thought you might be interested in some way.'

'In what way?'

'Something musical, a performance.'

'I don't do music.'

'Why?'

'It gets in the way and anyway the only musical type of thing that I would ever do is choral but I'm going to wait until I'm at least in my mid-50s before I start working on any choral things. In the meantime there's a stash of other stuff to be getting on with.'

'What kind of choral?'

'Look, I try not to let my mind think about it. It's too much of a distraction. I'm easily seduced. I only need to hear a John Tavener's Greek Orthodox mass or Russian monks chanting or even just The Sixteen on Radio Three. You do know The Sixteen?'

'Yeah.'

'Well anyway, as I said, I just need to hear some of that human voice vibrating with other human voices a fifth apart in a vague religious context and I want to ditch everything else and get composing minimal masterpieces for the new millennium. It gets silly.'

'You should do it.'

'NO. But...'

'But what?'

'You're from the Hebrides so you know what the Free Presbyterian Church is?'

'My father is a Minister in a Wee Free.'

'Perfect. Then you know exactly what I'm talking about.' And for you who don't, I will explain. The Wee Frees are a breakaway branch of the regular Presbyterian Church of Scotland. Their only stronghold is in the Gaelic-speaking Hebrides. They consider all forms of Presbyterian worship other than their own as a decadent corruption of the true way. As for any of the other forms of Christianity you might as well be an idol-worshipping pagan.

I like the Wee Frees. But then I didn't have to grow up with them dominating my life. My father was a minister in the aforementioned regular Presbyterian Church of Scotland. For me the Wee Frees were the exotic other.

What I liked and still like about their form of service best is they do not hold with any form of musical accompaniment when praising the Creator. They use only our God-given instrument, the voice. And, of course, they have no truck with those egocentric Victorian hymn-writing sluts. Even the prolific Wesleys don't get a look in. It is strictly the Book of Psalms used to provide lyrical content for their musical praise.

Instead of an organist or choirmaster leading the congregation in its musical direction, a man called the precentor leads the way. The precentor sings a line from a Psalm then the congregation repeats the line after him. Of course this means that it takes twice as long to get through any of the Psalms as it would normally take but this allows a competitive and improvisational tendency to develop in the way the precentor works his lines.

When the congregation joins in to repeat the line the precentor will improvise over the top of them. His instinctive need to impress either the Chief or Miss McLean in the fourth pew from the back will inspire him to greater leaps of artistic creation and spiritual depths of emotion.

White hipsters have spent at least the past five decades believing that it was only in the Afro-American tradition of singing that the great spiritual heights and depths can be reached – that whole 'black gospel choir spawning the only true voices of soul' line. It is not so much a lie, just a sad mistake made by all those who have never heard Donald McLeod lead the congregation through one of King David's Psalms sung in Gaelic.

So back to Norman Shaw and me standing outside Generator's HQ in Dundee.

'Perfect in what way Bill? I have a lifetime ahead of me with my family being unable to accept, let alone appreciate, what I do.'

'OK. I'm sorry. That's not what I meant. But what came into my head was the idea of the sound of a Wee Free congregation and precentor working their way through the twenty-third Psalm while inside that huge white golf-ball monument to global destruction. "Yeah though I walk through the valley of the shadow of death I will fear no evil."'

'What, as their fingernails start to glow?'

'Could be good. But I can't see any Wee Free congregation willing to go along with it.'

'Look Bill, I'm already late for work, I've got to go. Here's my number. Give me a call by the end of the week if you want to try and take this any further.'

Jonny Hanna, and one of the other lads gave me a hand loading up before we went for a pint in a local bar.

We talked about the employment available as a gallery attendant or technician in the recently opened Dundee Contemporary Arts. For a few hours a week they could earn enough to pay the rent, put bread on the table, a pint in the pot and buy time to get on with their own work.

'So what's it like at Dundee Contemporary Arts?'

'It's OK. We would be daft not to acknowledge that it has upped the profile of contemporary art in Dundee. Before it opened, the general population of Dundee had no awareness of art whatsoever. Now at least the local paper feels it has a responsibility to cover events and shows.'

'What kinda stuff do they show?'

'To be honest the regime there is in total thrall to the whole Britart glitterati. An artist could be working up in Scotland producing great work and a place like the DCA would not be interested. That same artist moves to London, gets written about in *frieze*, picked up by Jay Jopling or the Cabinet, bought by Saatchi, and 12 months later he or she will be offered a one-man show at the likes of the DCA.'

'But we all know that's always been the way. Scotland lacks the confidence to honour its own until London does it first.'

Time to move. I had to be in Aberdeen by 8.00 pm. Shook Jonny's hand, wished him all the best and was off. And it was back down to the Tay. I can never visit Dundee without going down to the waterfront to spend a couple of minutes just standing and staring out across the wide river. I always choose the same spot to do it. It's a couple of hundred yards up from where the rail bridge bends into the bank. There is a reason for this, and this is it.

We all love a good disaster. For some it's the historical kind, like the Titanic. For others, it's a need to see a famine or flood unfold nightly on the TV news. There's nothing like watching the six-year-old girl being dragged from the rubble eight days after the 'quake, her body broken but her heart still pumping. It doesn't matter how many thousands died in the initial shock, that one little girl's life being saved makes it all seem worthwhile. Then there is the African famine, the children with their distended bellies and the flies crawling over their faces so we can wallow in our collective guilt as we suppress the thought that life cannot be as precious to them as it is to us.

My favourite disaster is not one that I've witnessed, though I have witnessed upwards of 300 from a lifetime of daily news consumption. No, my fave' disaster happened late in the evening of 28 December 1879 and my only contact with it is from the reprint of a Victorian etching. It was also a modest disaster with only 75 fatalities as befits Scotland's status as a modest country.

Before the Tay Bridge with the bend in it was built there had been another one built a few years earlier. It reached the north bank of the Tay exactly where I do the standing and staring. The Edinburgh–Aberdeen train line had only recently opened. And on that fateful night of the 28th, the central arch of the old bridge collapsed under the weight of the Aberdeen-bound locomotive. The carriages obediently followed their engine down into the icy waters below. I'm not interested in the whys and hows, and who was to blame for it all, the fact that it happened is all I need to know.

As I've said before, I have a long-standing relationship with bridges. *Bridge Over the River Kwai* was my favourite war film. Other lads loved dinosaurs or weapons of mass destruction. For me it was always bridges. They filled me with awe and I always trusted they would take me to the other side. But any time I cross a bridge at night as a rail passenger my trust is tested. The horror of that winter night is alive and raging in me as if I'd seen it fresh on the news the night before.

But on that Wednesday evening I felt nothing. Usually I would get a rush of all sorts of vicarious sensations, like a Princess Di fan must get standing at the mouth of the Alma underpass in Paris. Instead my mind began to wander. It wandered into thinking about William McTaggart.

McTaggart is probably my favourite Scottish painter. The case of McTaggart is complete proof against what I said about Scotland lacking confidence to honour its own until London had first. If you don't know, McTaggart was a late Victorian painter. He used a broad and free-flowing brushstroke and in his time he was a superstar. But that stardom ended at the border. Within Scotland he was as big as

Constable or Turner had been. It was not crappy Monarch of the Glen stuff. He was truly modern. He could bring a Scottish landscape to life in a way that an Impressionist could do to a French one.

What's the worst form of provincialism — local stardom or not being recognised until being validated by those down the road? I don't know. So I put a placard up in honour of McTaggart. It went up on a post holding a lifebelt (not much use to the 75 who went down in the winter of 1879).

But as I did this my memory was jolted into thinking about an old man who lived half way up the hill, behind Nichol Logan's grocery shop, in my boyhood town of Newton Stewart. This old man was called Mr Agnew. Mr Agnew painted. My dad painted also but my dad painted watercolours. Mr Agnew painted in oils.

I remembered once coming up the hill on a warm summer afternoon from Nichol Logan's on my way home with messages for my mum. Mr Agnew's door was open. I heard a voice from within. 'Hello there, sonny. Are you Jack Drummond's wee lad?'

'Yes sir.'

'Well come in here and have a shifty at this painting I'm doing for the kirk. I want you to tell me what you think.'

'Yes sir.'

So I shyly shuffled in through the front door, down the passage and into the back room. Before I even got into the room I was almost overcome with this wonderful smell. Years later I learnt it was linseed oil. As I entered the room I was hit by a sight that I don't think any work of art has been able to muster since. Propped up on two easels was a massive canvas. When I say massive, I mean in the eyes of an eight-year-old boy who had never seen anything bigger than a regular watercolour. I suppose it was nothing compared to the size we expect to see in any contemporary gallery.

What was on the canvas was a wild seascape, mountains of clouds, shafts of sunlight. Actually, if I focus in on the memory, the sea wasn't storm-tossed or anything. The wildness came from the way the heavy paint had been applied. This wasn't the light brushwork of my dad's watercolours.

'So, what do you think to that sonny?'

'It's brilliant sir.'

'Do you know what it is?'

'The sea sir.'

'Aye, but do you know what that wee thing there is?' pointing to a couple of dabs of brown on the horizon.

'No sir.'

'That's a wee sailing ship back in the year 398AD and in that ship is Saint Ninian. Have you heard of Saint Ninian?'

'Yes sir.'

'Well, there he is, Saint Ninian, coming over the horizon, his destination in sight, bringing the Word to light our heathen land. Don't let anybody ever tell you that it was Saint Columba who brought Christianity over to Scotland first. Saint Ninian brought it over from Ireland, 165 years before Columba. He landed at the Isle of Whitorn, just down the road from here.'

'I know sir, I've been to his cave.'

'That's a good lad. Now, you run along and tell your faither I've nearly finished the painting.'

'Thank you sir. I will.' And I did.

I remember that this painting of Mr Agnew's took almost two years to complete. Where it was to hang had been the subject of much debate within certain quarters of the congregation. It would have been considered a bit papish to hang a painting celebrating a saint in the church itself (it being a Presbyterian kirk). The session room was too small. This left only the church hall, where it was hung over the fireplace. I used to sit in Sunday School, not listening to the teacher but staring up at Mr Agnew's finished painting and thinking, what if Saint Ninian had thought when he first saw the coast of Scotland and us lot standing on the beach, 'Fuck it, I'm not going there, it looks miserable and, anyway, they'll turn Christianity into this dour, dried up, dead religion. I'll go somewhere else instead.' Would we have all stayed heathens, building stone circles? I mean, I like stone circles, really like them, but it would have meant no Christmas, as in no Christmas presents. On balance I'm glad he came, anyway we can build stone circles as well. It doesn't have to be heathen. The mind of a nine-year-old child is a wonder to behold.

Twenty-odd years later I saw an almost identical painting to that of Mr Agnew's. It was called *Saint Columba Sailing Towards Scotland* and it was by William McTaggart. It didn't take anything away from my memory of Mr Agnew's painting. Obviously for a local painter in the tradition that Agnew was in, McTaggart must have been a hero. Agnew must have known the Saint Columba painting well. His sense of local pride would have inspired him to right this wrong in the nation's self knowledge. I put up another placard in honour of Mr Agnew and his back room filled with the smell of linseed oil and his kitchen table covered in tubes of paint.

Climbed back in the front seat, turned the key and headed out of town the long way round. Dundee always has a soothing effect on me. It seems to subtly turn internal cogs in a way different to visiting any other city. I also have some sympathy for its natives having to divide their loyalties between two football teams so that neither ever have the numbers in support to reach for any form of European glory.

The A90 between Dundee and Aberdeen is a grand road. Up and over the Sidlaw Hills. The gold was still pouring down from the sky and all over the Vale of Strathmore, the A90 swept around Forfar before heading north-east. If this had been a family jaunt I might have been tempted to take the coast road via Arbroath and Montrose but I was more than happy with this A90 as I tore past the turnings for Brechin City across the Howe of Mearns, over the bridges of Kair and Mondynes, stopping wherever the urge took me to fit a placard and take in a draught of the evening air.

And all the while in my head I could hear the sound of Donald McLeod and the congregation singing the words of David's twenty-third inside the dome at Dounreay. Who needs to get religion when you've already got it?

And, of course, the debate raged. Even British Nuclear Fuels had learnt the power to be sucked from contemporary art. Well not the power of the art but the value to be added by being seen to be supporting it. Nothing needed a makeover like the nuclear fuels industry, something to update its image. And nothing did it faster than contemporary art – ask Walsall or Salford. Back in the 1950s nothing was more modern than a man in a white coat talking about something you didn't understand. In 2000, nothing is more modern than a contemporary artist dressed in whatever they like talking about something you don't understand.

Actually I don't go along with what I've said in the last couple of sentences, I just wrote it for effect. All analogies are fundamentally flawed and only exist for the vanity of the person who is making them. Remember: never be swayed by an analogy.

What I was swayed by was the sight of Stonehaven. If I'd had the time I'd have turned off, driven down to the harbour, eaten fish and chips while I watched the trawlers get ready for the morning tide and their two weeks away from home, but no, I kept to the bypass and kept my foot on the floor. As I flew past the turning for New Mairns of Ury, I still had 15 miles to go. It was 7.35 pm. My eight o'clock show was to be my last and I was determined not to be late.

On this stretch of the A90 the North Sea is in view almost all the way. I like the heaviness of the North Sea. It is a no-messing-around kind of a sea. There it is, all along the eastern coast of Britain, and it doesn't do any of that ducking and diving behind scattered islands that some less trustworthy seas do. It doesn't need a sun setting in it to give it majesty, its solid greyness gives it all the regality a sea requires. There is nothing frivolous in its swell. No bounty to interest a be-hooked and velvet-clad pirate. No surfers have ever sought the perfect wave in its water. Nobody has ever worn a Hawaiian shirt as they strolled along its empty strands. There's just the cod waiting to be caught out on its Dogger Bank. And the odd pack of German U-boats to scare the shit out of an old coaster. When young men dream of running away to sea they don't dream of the North Sea.

In late 1998 I got sent a book in the post. It wasn't from amazon.com or a birthday present from my mum. There was no covering note, no explanation whatsoever. On its cover was a pizza delivery boy, his helmet visor still down, obscuring his face. In one hand he was carrying the pizza box wrapped up in a towel to retain heat. In his other hand was the chit. On his feet were a rather retro-looking pair of Adidas trainers. Its title was *Personal Delivery*, its author Duncan McLaren. I'd heard of neither before. I turned it over and read the blurb:

> Duncan McLaren – Gallery visitor, fiction writer, pizza delivery boy. He never/always compromises. In *Personal Delivery* he adds his own garnish to the deluxe pizza of contemporary art. Baked for eighteen months, 10-12 minutes and one terrifying second in the author's skidlid, at temperatures red hot to cool black, this book is a taste sensation – both an avant-garde concoction and a classical feast laden with Bonnes Bouches. Looking at the work of a variety of artistes, from the internationally acclaimed to those fresh out of art school, McLaren teases out the underlying ideas, often letting events in his own life – relations with the artist Jo Bennett and his experience as a writer - throw light on the artist's concerns.
>
> His uninhibited and imaginative responses go far beyond the academic or critical. Filled with lucid images, deadpan humour and challenging perspectives, *Personal Delivery* entices you into a thriving humane, multifarious world. Choose a shit sculpture. Follow bearded baby around the Isle of Sheppey. Live 'For Love of Today', wear a chastity belt for two months, inhabit a row of translucent polycarbonate cubicles, order a pizza, pret a lire style ... Cover design by Namara and the author. Cover photography by Oliver Zabat. ISBN: 07043 8091 9. Fiction/Non Fiction.
> (Autobiography, Contemporary Art) £12.

There was nothing else on the cover to read, so instead of going to the library to get on with my writing I sat down and read as much of this book as I could. My initial fear was that I had written the book under a pseudonym and forgotten all about it and here was the author's copy being sent to me.

The opening chapter of the book began with the line. 'To the Richard Long Exhibition at d'Offay's.' This was getting scary. How could one write a whole book and forget you have done it. I read on:

> Three stone circles made from blocks of slate have been installed. One can be stood inside; I step into it but don't linger. Another has a perimeter which is several blocks thick and would require a leap to be entered, a leap that would disturb the calm ambience here so I don't make it. The third is entirely infilled, jagged edges pointing upwards, and must be viewed from without. I walk round it, considering the red slate – some edges sliced straight by quarrymen or the artist – before turning to the gallery walls.
>
> Stone circles also appear in most of the half-dozen large, framed photos. I stand in front of a wide, flat New Mexican landscape; a lightly clouded sky over miles of featureless, scrubby desert. The circle of wayside stones in the foreground hardly dominates the scene. Does the presence of stone circles over the gallery floor encourage me to engage more with those the artist has assembled and photographed in New Mexico, Australia, Dartmoor and Iceland? Oh, I think it does.

Relief! I obviously hadn't written it. If you have already read my story 'A Smell of Money Underground' in *45* or elsewhere you will know that I am very much of the opinion that the presence of the stone circles over the gallery floor destroys any engagement I may have with the assembled photographs from Iceland or any other part of the world Long has gone to do his making.

So I guessed this Duncan McLaren or his publisher or publicist had noted that I too had written about Richard Long and thought I might have an interest in this book. Inspired by the book I wrote two short letters to the author, the first went:

> 'Dear Duncan,
> In my opinion, *Personal Delivery* contains the freshest approach to art criticism since Ruskin wrote *Modern Painters*.'

In the second letter I wrote:

'Dear Duncan,
In my opinion *Personal Delivery* is the most self-indulgent book purporting to be art criticism that I have ever read.'

Duncan McLaren wrote back, thanking me for my responses to his work. And that was that.

At least it was that until I was contemplating this drive up Britain. I had already sorted out the Glasgow stop off at Keith Farquhar's and the Dundee one at Generator and wanted to find somewhere else between Dundee to Dounreay. Someone had recommended I stop off at the legendary commune at Findhorn near Elgin but my internal prejudices told me 'Nah, that would be too hippyish.' Then I remembered that in the book *Personal Delivery* there had been a short chapter about visiting an art gallery on a farm somewhere near Peterhead. The trouble was I couldn't find the book anywhere in my house. I'd obviously lent it to someone. Instead I found the letter from Duncan McLaren. There was a phone number on the letter. I phoned. I got through to the author. He knew what I was talking about and gave me the name and number of an Iain Irving, curator and sole proprietor of the Greenwards by Hatton Gallery.

So I phoned Iain Irving. This was only a few days before this drive up Britain was to start and I explained about the *Personal Delivery* book and my vague memory of a chapter in it, what I was up to and the gap between Dundee and Dounreay. Iain Irving appreciated my problem but explained that the gallery in his house existed no longer but he had a notion that some of the post-grad and ex-students of the Aberdeen Art School had set up a place called Limousine Bull, an artist-run gallery space with much the same ethos as Generator. And he would ask. He did. And they were happy to ... So there I was flying over the Bridge of Dee at ten to eight, foot down on the brake, around the roundabout for the last exit. Fax copy of a hand-drawn map on my lap with directions of how to get to Limousine Bull. Everything was going fine, the windows were down, the balmy evening air welcoming me to the most well-scrubbed of all cities in the world. Nobody dislikes Aberdeen. There is nothing you can hold against it. Yes the Aberdonian is fabled to be the tightest in all of Scotland but you can forgive them that on account of their Doric dialect and sunny disposition. I was in the mood for sweeping generalisations – with all that crisp and glinting granite that the city is made from I felt confident in making them sweep.

Duthie Park to the left the Waters of Dee to the right. Along Riverside Drive, around a roundabout on to the North Esplanade West then turn right on to Market Street. Up until that point I had been able to keep all sense of nostalgia under control. My mind was focused on being on time for my final sales pitch. Then I saw the water, the evening sun dancing on the ripples, the trawlers tied up in the upper dock. I couldn't hold back the emotions anymore. I skidded up on to the pavement, leapt out clutching a brace of placards and attached them to the dock fence in honour of all those trawlers out riding the swell of the North Sea. What wouldn't I give to have been out there then, man against the elements, instead of being late for this last fray.

Well whatever it was I didn't give it. I pulled myself together, got back in the Land Rover and within five minutes was on Justice Street. It was a wide, clean edge of city centre street and according to the directions on my knee, was where Limousine Bull should be. Arty-looking people were spilling out on to the street from an open shop, talking and drinking red wine from plastic glasses. Iain Irving was there to greet me, all smiles and looks of relief that I'd actually made it. It had been converted from an old-fashioned grocer's shop. It was white-walled, moderate in size with a back office and a second exhibition space in the cellar. The place was packed.

'Do you want a hand in with your bits, Bill?'

'No thanks. I like doing it myself but I wouldn't mind a cup of tea.'

So I entered the place with my rolled-up carpet on my shoulder. I asked the people to move back as I did my by now well practised unrolling.

'We have a kettle but no plug Bill. Do you have a screwdriver we could use to take the plug off the projector to put on the kettle?'

'It's OK, I'll settle for a glass of water.' I got my other bits in. Leant them against the wall and then I began.

'Good evening. My name is Bill Drummond and I'm here this evening to make a sales pitch. What I would like to sell is...' and I was off, swaggering around my carpet, lifting my merchandise up at irreverent angles for all to see. My tongue was silver, my anecdotes burnished, my self-deprecating asides as finely tuned as Mika Hakkinen's Mercedes/Maclaren.

The crowd went from first-year art students up to lecturers considering what to do with early retirement. What was good about this bunch was that it wasn't just the usual couple of cocky lads who had a lot to say – just as many of the women were cutting in with their remarks and questions.

'However you wrap it up, however much you say or don't say, you're falling into the same trap as Richard Long. However pure his initial impetus, it is all negated by the commodification of his work. You are, almost by your own admission, on the same road.'

'But...' But I can't remember how I answered that one.

'All this about not knowing what you had bought is somewhat disingenuous of you. You know exactly what you bought and you don't like what it says about you. And now you want shot of it.'

'So what have I bought?'

'Porn.'

'I have never felt the need to buy porn in my life.'

'Well anybody who buys art not as an investment or to impress their friends or cheer the place up a bit is buying porn.'

'Porn. I'm not getting a hard on, are you?'

'You know what I mean. You are buying into something because you can't do it or get it yourself. You wouldn't buy porn if you could get all the perverted sexual kicks you desired for free with willing collaborators. There'd be no need. By buying this art you are buying into an experience at one remove. You are paying Richard Long to do it for you while you toss yourself off at his conceptual flights of fancy. Anthony d'Offay, the pimp; Richard Long, the whore; and you're the John. The trouble is you've sussed it and this *Smell of Sulphur in the Wind* is just a smutty magazine with the pages stuck together and now you want shot of it.'

This was getting good and then a man at the back cut in with a very simple and straightforward question, 'Do you own any other art?' A yes or no answer would have sufficed but I sidestepped the thrust of his question by giving the answer, 'Only a few bits and pieces by friends.' The trouble with this answer is the word 'friend', a word that can mean different things to different people.

As a person who prefers to spend as much time as possible in my own head, I've never quite been able to give up the childish habit of having fantasy friends. One of those friends is Monet. I like to chat with him in his garden while he paints his pond.

'Look Claude, why don't you give the painting a rest today? By my reckoning there is a giant pike lurking under those lily pads. What do you say we get ourselves a couple of rods and go after him?'

'You don't understand Bill, do you?'

And then there is me and Rothko.

'Look Mark, this stuff you're doing is going nowhere, it's boring. Cut out some magazine ads for Hoovers and Coca Cola and stick them on to your dreary washes of colour. You never know, it might be an artistic breakthrough. If you carry on like this it will drive you to suicide.'

'Suicide, that's a good idea Bill, that should seal my mythical status.'

'Fuck the myth-making, lighten up Mark. Let's get down The Cedar for a few beers.'

I do have some friends and I have got some art at home.

But anyway, more of that later. I got in my story about how I used to be based in Aberdeen back in 1974 when I was briefly an apprentice trawlerman on a boat working the northern waters. The show went well. The applause was genuine. Various offers were made to join the throng at various bars.

As I packed up, all offers of help were politely turned down. This too was all part of the show. Weave that myth boy, weave that myth. Two women offered to help. This was two women separate from each other. My ego felt ten-feet tall. Me need porn? Not likely son. With a rolled-up carpet like mine why would I ever need a dirty mag?

And I was off into the darkening sky in search of those northern lights and a single bed in some wayside inn.

But I got lost off Commercial Street, down by the docks. The street was empty but for a young lady with long blonde hair and micro-skirt. I slowed down to check her out, see if she was worth propositioning. My proposition was to be, 'Do you mind holding one of these "For Sale" placards love, while I take a photo of you?' But when I screwed up my eyes to get a better look at her, to see if she was worth the proposition, I realised I didn't have my specs on. Instant u-turn back up the guilty streets, around the bend and into Justice Street. Relief, there were still people clearing up and drinking the last dregs of wine. My specs were waiting for me faithfully by the glass of water.

Off across town again. Behind the drawn curtains I could imagine fathers reading their sons a bedtime story. 'Once upon a time, a long time ago there was a football manager who managed the lads up at Pittodrie Park. Those lads in red were the true Dons, they brought back European silver, something that Rangers have never done, never mind how many times they have won the league.'

'But Dad, why doesn't he still manage the reds?'

'He does son, they just happen not to be our reds.'

'But whose reds are they, Dad?'

'Manchester United's, son.'

Poor boy, his dad reads him the same story every night and every night he wonders if he could ever tell his dad that he secretly supports Manchester United.

I stopped on a tree-lined street to stick up a placard outside a granite house with the curtains shut in honour of the Don's glory days. I stuck up another one, hoping the snap would capture the last lingering light of the day. This one was in honour of Billy Lyndsey, an Aberdonian and follower of the Dons. Billy was the first in our class to jack in the sixth form. His first weekly wage packet was four pounds, nineteen shillings and sixpence (£4/19/6d), as a trainee quantity surveyor.

He was also the first of us to father a child.

The A96 out of town. I was hoping to make Inverness before I turned in but just a couple of miles further up the road and I was falling asleep at the wheel. They may not have been the Northern Lights but the lights of Aberdeen Airport looked mighty fine to me. They drew me in and, waving my credit card, I checked into the biggest airport hotel on offer, ordered a half-bottle of Cabernet Sauvignon and some seafood pasta dish on room service, tried to phone Sallie to hear how she and the family were but fell asleep before my meal and wine arrived.

I woke up. It was still dark. The hum of the air conditioning began to frighten me. There was a voice in my head.

'Do you own any other art? I said, do you own any other art? Mr Drummond, are you listening? DO YOU OWN ANY OTHER ART?'

'Yes I'm listening.'

'Well do you? And don't give me any of that bollocks about Monet and Rothko. You don't have imaginary friends, you just made that up for effect. A yes or no answer is what I require.'

'Look, didn't you read that story in *45* where I went off to buy that advert thing to cure myself of the need to buy art?'

'Yes.'

'So?'

'So you still haven't come clean with me, have you?'

'Fuck off and let me go back to sleep. I've got an early start you know.'

'Yes I know but a little birdy tells me you've got a couple of Richard Billinghams hanging in your house. Can you explain this?'

'So what?'

'So what! A lot of people think the idea of the art-buying classes spending thousands on photographs depicting the dysfunctional goings-on in the Billingham household is an abomination of taste. Hanging these pictures of fat Liz and alckie Ray on their walls for their friends to admire when they come round for a dinner party is about as sad and sick as the art market can get.'

'Of course I know that.'

'So why aren't you getting rid of these pictures as well as or at least instead of the Richard Long one? Are you afraid of what your dirty little secret tells the world about you?'

'Well firstly, I bought them as gifts for my girlfriend, Sallie, and our daughter, Tiger. They own them, I'm not in a position to sell them.'

'You're dodging the issue.'

'No I'm not. I'm just getting to it. As I've said before, I've got no on-going relationship with the Richard Long picture, it doesn't engage me. If art doesn't engage you, it has no worth. Every day the two Richard Billingham photos we have hanging in our house engage me. They work. They do their job. I'm getting my money's worth.'

'Work? Doing their job? Money's worth? Mr Drummond, what kind of far-fetched reasoning is this?'

'Every morning I come downstairs and I've got to go through our living room to get to the kitchen. On our living room wall is a big print of Liz reclining on her grubby settee in her flat somewhere in the redundant West Midlands, surveying our spacious living room somewhere in the home counties. And Liz is not some fiction in an artist's head, she is living, breathing, dealing with life, not a Henri Cartier-Bresson black and white image from a now-mythical past or a chic portrait of a Nan Goldin cross-dressing heroin-shooting friend, dying of Aids. It's a here and now, just up the M1 thing. Liz is putting on the kettle as I put on the kettle. She is feeding her dogs and cats as I feed ours. If Liz died then there might be no reason for having her up. The force of the picture would change. It would become history, as in redundant. Like a picture of the Queen on the wall of your local British Legion – as soon as she dies it will no longer work and will have to be replaced by a picture of Charles. "The king is dead, long live the king" and all that. The fact they are both called Liz is a bonus.'

'But Mr Drummond, the commodification of someone else's misfortunes for your entertainment is as sick as contemporary art can get.'

'You said that before and anyway you are again stating the obvious. That's what gives it power. Whether Richard Billingham as the artist intended that is irrelevant. The whole notion of Richard Billingham taking pictures of his own white-trash family and selling them for a considerable profit gives this stuff more potency. Most art that gets produced is far too self-aware to work. There is very little friction within it. So often it is just a display of wit and intelligence. Most art doesn't fuck with your head. It just pats it and says, "Aren't you clever, you get it too." It's all been worked out before we see it. Even if the artists pretend to themselves to be innocent in all of this, that too is all part of the game that they are selling and what we are buying.'

'You're over-stating it, Drummond. There is a lot of art being made out there that isn't just a display of wit and intelligence for those who get it, to indulge in. There's still no need to go and buy the stuff.'

'Look, if you really want to know it gets worse, far worse and that's why I like it even more. I've got a friend, a photographer, whose name is Paul Graham. He saw some of Billingham's photos in a group show at the Barbican back in 1994. This was Billingham's first show outside of the West Midlands and since leaving art school. The show was called 'Who's Looking At The Family.'

'Paul introduced himself to Billingham at the opening of this Barbican show, told him that if he was down in London again to look him up. Billingham did, and a loose working relationship evolved. Billingham had no gear, he got his photos developed at the local Boots using the cheapest film he could find. Paul had top gear. Paul introduced Billingham's work to Anthony Reynolds, the owner of the gallery that represents Paul. Reynolds recognised the commercial possibilities of Billingham's family snaps. Paul printed up Billingham's snaps to the large-scale format that has become the norm since photographs first began to be marketed as contemporary art. Photos as big as paintings to compete in the white-wall wars and all that well documented stuff.

'Now I could have got myself some offcuts from Paul's studio floor or even (maybe) a reject print before Paul tore it up and flung it in the bin. I could have Blu-Tacked these offcuts or rejects to my wall, sat around of an evening admiring my smart arse and polishing my cynical overview of it all. Who wants to be part of the solution when you can be part of the problem is what I say.'

'Is this some sort of rationale for being an arms trader?'

'OK. OK. I'll get back to the subject in hand, me buying art. So when Anthony Reynolds put on Billingham's first one-man show, I was down there like a shot, got my orders in before the free wine was being handed around and the peanuts munched.'

'So that's your story. You can go back to sleep now.'

'No. Not quite. Much has been written about Charles Saatchi's position within the contemporary art world, where he buys the market follows, etc. Well, I would like to take this opportunity to brag that I bought my one of the edition of five prints of Liz reclining on her sofa before Saatchi bought his. That while the hundreds of thousands of punters were trooping past Liz reclining in all her glory like Manet's *Olympia* at the 'Sensation' show back in 1997, there she was hanging on my living-room wall, escalating in value. While in reality she was up in the West Midlands putting on the kettle again and I'm already sitting down to sup my second cup. Don't you just love it?'

'Are you quite finished?'

'No! There is something else. Christmas 1998, Paul Graham sent me a gift. It was a big print of a photo he had taken for Jimmy and me. The photo was of the brick we had made from the ashes of the money we had burnt. It looked good but what was even better was what he had wrapped it in. It was one of the reject Billingham prints. This meant I could have my cynical overview and be part of the mess at the same time. Anyone for this piece of cake I've already eaten?'

'You're a wanker Drummond.'

And on that summation of my character I fell asleep.

I had asked a friend, Chris Brook, who is featured earlier in this tale, to read through what I had written and give me his criticisms. The following is what he wrote about the whole 'voice in my head/ Billingham' bit.

'I think this is the major weakness in the tale so far. It's suffocatingly self-referential and like you've contrived a situation to start a rant which is actually something else. Cut it down substantially? Refer to it differently? I think the waking up in the hotel and salient issue of owning this art is OK. But… for the first time something is jutting out oddly and not working. It's like you've slid an art theory essay in here under dubious disguise.'

Chris Brook has rumbled me. It had been shoved there, there was no voice in my head. In fact I never woke up. Had a sound night's sleep.

But I'm not going to take his advice. It stays as I wrote it.

Into the Flow

8 June 2000

The wake-up call went off at 6.30 am. I was out on the road with a full tank of diesel by 6.50 am. The plan had been to make the visitors' centre at Dounreay by the time it opened at 10.00 am.

Something I have just remembered. It was while I was checking into the airport hotel that I stumbled on how to work the date and time thing on the camera that appears on the bottom right-hand corner of the pictures. Thus explaining the lie that all the pictures so far in the book were taken in March 1998.

The A96 holds little charm for me. Just a boring, winding A road through some middling Scottish countryside. Even the knowledge that this countryside contained more ancient stone circles than anywhere else in the world could not detain my imagination. Mind you, I was tired and just wanted to get the job done. Still, I did stop off and stick up a few placards on the way. What I did to amuse myself over these dull miles was to indulge myself in one of my stand-by fantasies. The fantasy is that one day I will own a tea room. The Penkiln Burn Tea Rooms will be its name and it's where I will spend my twilight years, making vats of soup, baking cakes and brewing large pots of tea for weary travellers. And, of course, I'll be spinning yarns for anyone who cares to listen, about how it used to be in the old days. On the walls will hang my trophies. In the corner will be a juke box playing my favourite hymns, and on the floor I will have a carpet with the words 'Tea Room' in it. This carpet will be exactly the same style and size as the 'For Sale' one but in dark brown.

As with any fantasy there has to be a certain number of variables to keep it fresh. With this fantasy the variable is its location. Sometimes The Penkiln Tea Rooms is in a Peruvian village high in the Andes.

Other times it is in a shack out somewhere across the Norfolk Fens. On the morning of 8 June 2000 The Penkiln Tea Rooms was on a light industrial estate in Milton Keynes, between a maker of extractor fans and a constructor of those three-wheeler off-road baby pushchairs. Maybe I should tour the tea room. I stretched the fantasy out all the way to Inverness by composing my fantasy menu.

As the A96 swerved into the A9 my fantasy came crashing down at the sight of the Inverness Caledonia Thistle's Football ground. This football ground was a brand-new affair and built right by the dual carriageway. I knew very little about Inverness other than what you learn in history books.

For a start, I didn't know what the best supermarket in town was or where you had to go to get your drug of choice. It was where I had the worst curry in my life but that was back in 1982 with Dave Balfe when he had an imaginary band called the Turquoise Swimming Pools. Things might have improved on the curry front since then, as for the Pools they never evolved from their imaginary stage.

Back to the Caledonia Thistle football ground. I had an instant urge to burn it down. When I was at a secondary modern in Corby we played shinty. Shinty is a game like hockey but cruder, native to the Highlands of Scotland. It's a great game to play, fast and furious. I've never understood why it hasn't caught on in farther fields. The shinty stick is made from a three-foot switch of hazel, steam-bent at the head. These were easy to make or cheap to buy. As for the ball, a knackered golf ball did the job. Inverness is a sizeable city as far as cities in Scotland go, a big enough city to support a Scottish Premier football club but Inverness was also the capital of the shinty-playing world. The good folk of Inverness were not to be seduced by the monied glamour of soccer as played by the wicked south.

Now I don't know anybody from Inverness or if what I say has ever been really true, but it's what I held faith with. I know what I'm about to say contradicts what I said about football when I was going on about that book Posts, but I like to believe that there are pockets of the world, pockets even in our own islands, that can withstand the onslaught and globalisation of football. I know I come on at times like the rich tapestry should be thrown on the bonfire and be done with it. 'One world, one game' always seems like an attractive step to eternal world peace. How could we go to war against a people we play football against, and all that?

Maybe this drive up Britain was more an excuse to air a corner of the rich tapestry for my inspection than a sales pitch. An excuse for me to indulge in the broad sweeps and blurred edges of this land at this turn of the calendar, at this tick of my internal clock.

Night after night we see that outline of our island while the weather girl tells us about cold fronts and warm spells which might or might not visit our shores on the morrow. We might not believe her forecast but we take it on faith that Britain is all there, from Cornwall to Caithness; from Dover to Duncansby Head. But is it? How do we know? So I've been checking it out, making sure the full distance is there, from the bottom to the top.

I'm not very good at advising people on things. In the past when I've attempted to do it, the advice has usually been fundamentally flawed for some obvious reason that I overlooked at the time.

I'm going to risk the imminent arrival of a fundamental flaw and advise you to take a drive up Britain at least once in your life. Of course you make your own route, you don't have to drive, you can hitch it, bus it, train it, but don't walk or bike it. If you walk it or bike it, it all becomes about something else, it gets into those dodgy areas like raising money for charity or proving how fit you are or, even worse, looking to give your life purpose. No, it serves no other purpose than to check that it is actually there, from Southampton to Dounreay.

Maybe that's why Muslims make sure they go to Mecca once in their life. Every day they get their rug out and say their prayers facing Mecca but how do they know it's there? Can you really trust your brother when he comes back from his hadj? You've got to go yourself, all those prayers might have been in vain. So instead of going to wherever it is you go for your summer holiday, take a trip up this stretch of land one year.

Anyway, back to shinty and Inverness Caledonia Thistle. A few seasons back, it was decided that if the two very minor football teams of Inverness Caledonia and Inverness Thistle were combined and some money was shoved in, a commercially successful football team could be created. Sadly, that appears to be happening. It seems that each successive season Caledonia Thistle climbs a division. This season (2000/2001) they will be knocking on the door of the Scottish Premier division. All very healthy for the investors of the club but where did that leave shinty? Less chance than ever of young lads in Inverness dreaming of being top-grade shinty players.

Does this matter? And who gives a fuck? Well at times, like the time I drove past the almost spanking new Inverness Caledonia Thistle football ground, I felt like I did. For the ten seconds it took for me to drive past it, that ground symbolised the dark underbelly of that behemoth we call democracy whose wings only flap when the strings are pulled by a distant few.

Ten seconds only last as long as they do and I was soon on to the bridge with Beauly Firth to the west and the Moray Firth to the east, all thoughts of global media conspiracy lifted. The Land Rover swung on to the Black Isle. No more than ten minutes later and I was on another spectacular bridge crossing the Cromarty Firth back on to the mainland. For the next 15 miles the A9 runs along the edge of Cromarty Firth. What's great about this stretch of road is that you can play count the oil rigs.

Oil rigs get dragged from out where they do their drilling for black gold on the watery wastes of the North Sea into the almost landlocked, calm waters of Cromarty Firth to be refitted. Or at least I guess they are being refitted, maybe they just go there for rest and recreation. Anyway you can usually count at least a dozen of these monsters scattered up this Firth between Alness Bay and Nigg Bay. Usually when I drive up this stretch of the A9, I count the oil rigs hoping to beat my 1983 record when I spotted 19 of the monsters.

But on this morning the sight of the rigs did not fill me with awe. I wasn't even bothering to count them. Stuck to the dashboard of the Land Rover I keep a small lump of Blu-Tack. You never know when you might need a bit of Blu-Tack and the dashboard seems as good a place as any to keep it. That's the justification, the real reason I had it there was to play with. Some have rosary beads, some pick their noses, others smoke, I have my small lump of Blu-Tack. Between the thumb and forefinger of my left hand I incessantly roll it round, trying to create the perfect sphere. In circumference it's no bigger than a ten-pence piece but on that Thursday morning the 15 oil rigs resting and recreationing on Cromarty Firth could not compete with my ball of Blu-Tack. This, I think, had more than something to do with the art of Martin Creed. Martin Creed is the artist whose first 15 minutes of fame will be remembered for his ball of waste paper.

So there I was, passing the turn-off for Invergordon, ignoring the oil rigs, looking at my ball of Blu-Tack, wondering how the pubic hair got stuck in it and wondering if Martin Creed had got himself his own ball of Blu-Tack or whether I should send him this one. And I was thinking, 'Well is that the power of art? Somebody comes along and presents the world with a ball of screwed-up waste paper and I can no longer be impressed by 19 huge oil rigs dragged in from the North Sea.' I treasure moments like that and you somehow know that the power of that ball of waste paper isn't just to do with hype for the latest wave of whatever they call it. Something else is going on. It can be these little things that shift the way we see the world. Martin Creed is a prime example of an artist who was only taken to heart in Scotland once he had been lionised in London. They are probably planning a Martin Creed show at Dundee Contemporary Arts as I write this story.

In fact, that has just brought something into focus for me.

I'm bored with big art. I'm usually the last to get bored with something. So if I'm bored, most other people must be. Big art just looks old-fashioned, past its sell-by date. Hanging about and cluttering up the place, trying to impress you. We need a clear out.

Oh shit, I can feel a new manifesto coming on. I can't stop myself, here it comes skittering down my trousers. Looks like it's called 'The Open Manifesto'. That sounds as good a title for a manifesto as any other. Not least 'cause it has the inclusive ring of the Open University which fits in with my on-going infatuation with all things Milton Keynesian. The Open Manifesto exists for anybody to add to with their own new doctrines, dogmas or principles. The first rule is that from now on nobody should make art that is any bigger than themselves. The second rule is that people who take photographs should try and resist exhibiting their prints any larger than the standard format you get back from Boots.

If you have any doctrines, dogmas or principles you would like added to The Open Manifesto, please send it to open@penkiln-burn.com and it will be added to the list. Please state whether you do/don't want to be credited with your entry. And try to make sure it's a new, never-been-tried-before one. The Open Manifesto won't want any old, worn-out dogmas. There is no time limit. Send in whatever quantity you like, history will deal with the quality.

For The Open Manifesto to work, it would be better if you believed in what you are saying. Even if you personally will find it difficult to live by your own rules. No jokes. Keep it as irony-free as you can. I know that's hard in this day and age. This could run and run or fizzle out by next week, just another ill-attended website, another meaningless message board. I hope it will last at least as long as my lifetime. An ever growing week-by-week, month-by-month, year-by-year manifesto. Always on the move. Up to the moment. Setting 1000 agendas for whatever is to happen next.

As I swerved around the roundabout at the turning for Nigg Ferry and headed north for Tain, my mind drifted on from the ball of Blu-Tack, Martin Creed and The Open Manifesto. It was shifting back through all that renaissance of Scottish art business. How long before it burns out and the focus shifts? 'Has Douglas Gordon burned out?' I asked the windscreen wipers. The windscreen wipers only replied in a way that smeared all the dead moths and midges across my windscreen without clearing the light shower of rain that just fell.

I checked into that section of my brain that was still playing *100-Hour Psycho*. It was boring, so I switched off the motor of the projector leaving the heat from the projector light to melt the celluloid thus destroying the one and only copy that exists of the film inside my head.

Time flew by, as did Morangie, and I was zooming over Dornoch

Firth heading up for where the A9 skims the edge of Loch Fleet. Although my mind had left *Psycho* behind, it was still stuck in a Douglas Gordon rut. This time I was on to that 'list of all the people he has ever known' thing he does. I like that. I think it's epic. It's a game we all play from time to time in some way. For me, it used to be how many of the names and faces of the other children I could remember who were in my primary one class back in 1958. Six years ago I could remember all 41 of them, now I can only recall 11. I tried to console myself by the thought that this proof of my failing memory meant nothing to me as I'm not really a people person. A social life would be wasted on me. Even if I had one I wouldn't know what to do with it. How about trying to remember how many roads I had ever driven down? By the time I passed Dunrobin Castle just after Golspie, I decided this task was too easy. It was also boring. I could recall every road I had ever driven down in my life, so I changed subject to pots of tea. How many places could I recall drinking a pot of tea in? This, as a subject, connected with something vague and deep in me – each pot of tea I could recall marked a small shift, a slight tilt in the course of my life. I'm tempted to quote that infamous quote of Boy George's but I won't. It would not be true. Sex can fuck your life up, tea can't. I was all for lives getting fucked up — makes for more interesting art and all that.

As tea is such a subtle drug we don't usually register its effects whereas coffee is obvious, bangs you straight between the eyes and gets you shuddering. For me starting the day without a pot of tea would be a day forever out of kilter.

There was a house by the side of the road in Portgower that looked like it was straight out of an Alfred Wallis painting, so I stopped and stuck a placard on it. I then got back to counting teapots. I got to 316 pots in different places by the time the Land Rover was hurtling down the road into Helmsdale. I pulled up at the bridge, attached one of the placards to a lamp post in the middle of the bridge, then had a look at the enamelled Michelin map.

Look, I've got to come clean with you. I lied. I didn't have an enamel-on-steel map on the seat next to me. I didn't unscrew one from Ray's door and leave that note through his letterbox. What happened was this.

I've long wanted one of those maps. Last week I asked Ray how I could get one, hoping he'd offer me his rusting one for a couple of quid. He told me Michelin come round every six or seven years, take the old one down and put a new one up.

'You should just come along one night Bill and nick mine.' It was a jest.

'So can I buy it off you, Ray?'

'No, I need it for when people stop and ask me for directions. You can have it when Michelin come around to give me a new one again.'

'When might that be?'

'A couple of years.'

'I need one for next week as a prop for a thing I'm doing.'

And then somebody pulled up for an oil change and Ray had to get back to work and I got off. I put in a call to Michelin but they wouldn't sell me one and I couldn't bring myself to nick Ray's.

Time to turn off the A9 on to the A897. I was going into the unknown. This was a road I had never ever driven along in my entire life. Virgin territory and all that. Right from the start I knew this would be epic. The weather was miserable in the most perfect of ways. No torrential rain or great shafts of sunlight, just drizzle and greyness. There was that kind of midday non-light that makes everything seem small and meaningless. Definitely not the kind of light that stirs the loins of movie makers. The signposts promised me 40 miles of unbroken single-track road with occasional passing places. 'Drive with care — lambs on road', a shepherd had painted on the side of a huge but redundant tractor tyre for us to heed. Of course I read this as a message from the Almighty. Similar to the one He had given Abraham when he was about to slaughter his son, Isaac, as an offering.

As you may remember, the Chief said, 'OK Abraham, I believe you're willing to slaughter your only son because I told you to. You don't need to bother, instead slaughter this lamb that's stuck in yon briar.'

And that was that. It was quite a simple command for Abraham to follow. This one I was being presented with was a bit more complex. Bit of a riddle in fact.

My instinct was to drive as fast and as recklessly as possible along those 40 miles of single track road, safe in the knowledge that around any bend could be an oncoming tractor and I would catapult myself into the arms of the Holy Spirit as a mangled offering. But instead of Him saying, 'OK Bill, I believe you're willing to squander your only life because I told you to, you don't need to bother, you can run down this lamb a few miles up the road instead.' He is saying 'slow down, son 'cause I don't want you to kill the lamb.' So if the lamb doesn't get killed and I don't get killed as a by-product of the lamb not getting killed, who gets killed? Where was the offering?

If you're wondering, 'How come Drummond lets his mind career down these biblical back roads?' and 'Who in this day and age is impressed with a working knowledge of the Bible?' I don't have an answer but hindsight is at hand with a few nods and winks and wanting to have a say. I'm writing these notes a few weeks after the journey. In front of me on the table are two of the photos I took, the one with the big tyre and the one with the signpost 'Melvich 40 miles'. Looking at these photos now reminds me of a maxim I like to use: never trust poetry. Poetry has a sneaky and shifty way of working. On first reading, the words seem innocent enough, the rhymes cute, the metre in step but then they get to work inside your head, inciting emotions best left to rest. The poet is usually as innocent as you the reader of the real power of what s/he is putting on paper. Even single words have so many hidden meanings that can never be articulated, internal rhymes that can kick-start urges that have lain dormant since childhood.

These two photos are working on me like a poem can. That number 40 on the signpost must have kick-started the avalanche of internal symbolism. Even if your knowledge of the Bible is sketchy you will know that the number 40 is only used when the Israelites or some other biblical characters have to confront some big issue.

So it was for 40 days and 40 nights that it rained, bringing Noah his flood.

It was for 40 years that the Israelites wandered the wilderness.

It was 40 days and 40 nights that Moses spent up the mountain.

Forty stripes of the lash was the favourite non-capital punishment of the Old Testament.

And, of course, it was 40 days and 40 nights that Jesus spent in the wilderness before starting his job as the Saviour of Mankind, in fact, the Lamb of God.

This 40 miles of the A897 I was about to drive traversed an area called the Flow Country. The Flow Country is famed among British lovers of nature as the last true wilderness we have in this land. It's that most biblical of words 'wilderness' that is always used to describe the Flow Country in any nature book you choose to pull from your shelf. And what was it flowing with? Tears? Milk? Blood? Honey? Or Class A Peat Bog? So it was to be 40 miles on a single-track road through a wilderness flowing with something or other to a place called Melvich. That hindsight was now turning the name Melvich around in my brain. Was it its obvious internal rhyme with the word 'hell?'. Was it because it sounded like Melville as in *Moby Dick*, as in 'Call me Ishmael', as in Abraham's bastard son who was sent out into the wilderness (that word again) with his mother, Hagar? Hindsight tilts the name Melvich around a bit further and the name Moloch comes tumbling out.

After the Israelites spent their 40 years in the wilderness and came to the land flowing with milk and honey, they had to overcome a people known as the Canaanites. The Canaanites worshipped an idol called Moloch. Moloch required his people to offer him children in sacrifice. So much tastier than lambs.

Look, it's not that I hold with any of this biblical stuff but it's all rattling around inside. It's part of who we are as much as Nasty Nick in Big Brother and Patsy leaving Liam or whatever tabloid bollocks you are reading this week.

So I put my foot down on the accelerator in the hope that I would slaughter a lamb before I killed myself. A couple of miles out along this single-track road with the windows down and all the biblical-Bill bollocks was well and truly blown back where it belonged.

Although I had never travelled along this road before I had

cut across the Flow Country a couple of times in my youth. A true wilderness, which only a far ocean or distant desert could rival. I've tried to keep the observation of wildlife out of these notes. If I didn't, they would run to several volumes.

As a card-carrying member of the RSPB, I am very well aware of how the Flow Country is constantly endangered by commercial afforestation, thus the habitat of some of our most rare and alluring bird types. A few pairs of greenshanks had been known to breed on the Flow but it was the whimbrel that I was hoping to spot. The whimbrel is a close relative of the curlew but vastly more scarce. It has the same wader's legs, brown and cream flecked feathering, long and elegantly curved beak. It is only the crown of the whimbrel that marks him in his outward appearance to be different to the curlew. The whimbrel has a couple of dark stripes across his dome, the curlew none. I understand its melancholic song is different as well. The truth is that even if I saw a whimbrel at less than a few feet in front of me I would not know for sure if s/he was the real thing.

The road curved down into a scattered settlement. I flew past a sign saying Kinbrace. The name was familiar, was it a friend from school? The name of an ancient battle field? Or just one of the other names on that signpost that had 'Melvich 40' on it? Then I remembered — Kinbrace was the centre of the Scottish gold rush of '69 (that's 1869).

I instantly had visions of dumping everything to make my fortune panning for gold in the streams thereabouts. Then it came back to me that I had already made and squandered it. The vision evolved into something else and as it did I remembered someone telling Jimmy and me a fortnight before we did the squandering that it was a fruitless task as Yves Klein had already thrown gold into the Seine and in art it was only the first person to paint the Mona Lisa that gets the credit. At the time we thought, 'Fuck Yves Klein, we want to burn it anyway.' But since then there has always been that niggling sense of resentment against Klein and his flinging into the Seine.

So as I tore past these few scattered houses that comprised Kinbrace a thought struck me. I bet Yves Klein never panned for his own gold. I bet he just got it off a Parisian gold merchant or art collector. I would pan for my own gold in the clear silver streams of the Flow, take it up to Dounreay, scatter it into the sea and watch it glitter and glow green in the radiating waters as it sunk to the nuclear-rich sediments. But I didn't.

A few miles north of Kinbrace and it was the Flow proper. One thousand scattered lochs. Land that's never been farmed, useless even for grazing sheep. I pulled up, switched off the engine, climbed out and just stood and stared at whatever it is we stare at when we are overcome by nature. I could hear a curlew call. I didn't dare to even think it could be a whimbrel.

Then a flock of smallish waders landed a few yards from me. It was as if they hadn't seen me. I had to flick through the waders section of *The Reader's Digest Field Guide to the Birds of Britain* that I have lodged in my brain like a Muslim has the Koran. Page 122, Golden fuckin' Plover. There, just feet from where I was standing was a flock of Golden Plover. Now the Golden Plover is reasonably widespread. Any bit of northern moorland and you have a chance of seeing one, but I never had. This was a first for me. Not that I'm a notebook-ticking twitcher but all birds for me are angels. If angels are going to have feathery wings, why would they bother with having the bodies of men? Birds as angels, it's so much easier to get your head around.

You've heard of the Four Horsemen of the Apocalypse, well the Flow Country is the sort of place you could imagine them galloping across. Now I don't give a shit for the four horsemen, never liked the Book of Revelations. What I hold with is the four golds of the *Atlas of Breeding Birds in Britain & Ireland* (1988–91 consensus): the Gold Crest, the Gold Finch, the Golden Eagle and the Golden Plover. The golden eye doesn't count because there is nothing gold about it and the golden pheasant is an exotic import. Who needs to pan for a mere metal, however unbase, when you can see and watch the real thing? Gold, the metal, may have symbolised many things across the world for thousands of years but did that golden calf have the breath of God in it when Moses came down the mountain after he had done his 40 days and 40 nights? Course it fuckin' didn't. But those Golden Plovers had the breath of God flowing through to the very tips of their wings.

Now if Yves Klein had wanted to be clever he would have forgotten all about charging a Parisian art collector to throw a mere metal into the Seine. He'd have said, 'Look mate, give me a million francs and come with me up to the Flow Country and I will show you pure 40,000 carat gold fly across the sky.'

I got back in the Land Rover. This called for a celebration of sorts. This requires me to reveal to you another sordid and shameful secret of mine. Under the driver's seat of the Land Rover I keep a cassette. My family don't know it's there, I've never played it when any passenger was on board. I do try to limit the amount of times I use it but some things are very hard to give up. You will have gathered that I'm very anti the past. If I had my way all music more than a year old would be wiped.

Old music just encourages nostalgia, even worse, it fosters classicism. All music should be the first music. All music should be created while floundering around in a state of flux with no direction known.

In fact I have a new dogma to add to The Open Manifesto. You should only listen knowingly to music released in the year when you're listening. And the music must be the debut recording by the artist or group.

I found the cassette under my seat among the old chip wrappers, used notebooks and my dad's army issue of the Bible. Its cover had long since been discarded and its label obliterated by the ink of a black felt-tip pen. *Bob Dylan's Greatest Hits.* I wished I didn't need to, I wished I could throw it out of the window along with my suitcase full of cassettes by Elvis and George Jones and Al Green and Hamilton Bohannon and Miles Davis and Muddy Waters and Fairport Convention and Iggy Pop and Kraftwerk and Chic and the Petshop Boys and Public Enemy and Bert Jansch and Best of UK Garage 1998.

But no, there it was in my hand and I shoved it in, turned up the volume to distort and got going before anyone could stop me. And bang, straight into It's *All Over Now Baby Blue* somewhere near the end of side one and I was feeling better than any man ought to feel. I've never been arsed about lyrics of songs. Never read a lyric sheet in my life. As for Bob Dylan's words, I couldn't quote you more than two consecutive lines and I don't give a fuck what they meant when he wrote them. But I sangalongaBob at the top of my voice, every sneering, leering, whining line.

Look, I do wish it wasn't like this, that I wasn't from the arse-end of a generation who venerated this toss-pot. I wish my little secret was a cassette of music by somebody the world had not heard of instead of the ultimate icon of every ageing *Guardian*-reading, faded liberal. At least I've not gone to see him live since the 1969 Isle of Wight Pop Festival.

The odd lines of his lyrics that I do recall take on different meanings every time I hear them. So on that June day Baby Blue was obviously Yves Klein. If you have a smattering of knowledge of twentieth-century art, you might not recall his scattering of gold on the Seine but you will know that Klein was the King of Blue. 'Blue has no dimension, it is beyond dimensions whereas other colours are not...' Of course he was right, but as of today it's all over now Baby Blue.

There was not one square inch of blue in that Flow Country sky. The whole lot was grey. Now there is an idea I should start marketing, a range of paints all of which are shades of grey, 'Drummond's International Grey'. 'Sorry sir, only matt, no gloss. The boss says that gloss reflects, thus ruining the purity of the greyness.'

Just north of Dalhalvaig I pulled up and stuck a placard on the railing surrounding a granite war memorial. Back in the Land Rover I turned the cassette over and got going again, 'Gimpo's in the basement mixing up the medicine...' And why was 'the pump don't work 'cause the vandal's took the handle' my all-time favourite Dylan line? Maybe it was a sign that I should start stealing petrol pump handles. As the Land Rover tore past Achiemore I was screaming.

> 'I've got everything I need.
> I'm a liar
> and you can't play.
> I can fade the night time
> and paint the daytime grey.'

The road came to a shuddering end. If I turned left, it would take me across the bridge into Melvich. If I turned right along the A836, I was only seven miles from my final destination of Dounreay nuclear power station.

I got out of the Land Rover and kissed the tarmacadam of the A897 goodbye. I cannot recommend this less travelled road too highly. If you want to get your psychogeographical kicks, this is the place to come. Forty miles of breathtaking insanity, staggering instability, a place where the rhymes of reason will be left untied, unmetered and unwanted, to wriggle in their death throes.

I pulled the Richard Long out the back and laid it down on the verge. It looked good there. Then the clouds shifted, letting a few rays of sunlight splash the landscape. This made the picture look even better. The camera was hanging around my neck and before I could call on my better judgement I was taking a picture of it lying there.

Then, clearly under the influence of David Hockney's photo montage pictures, I decided to see if I could make myself a patchwork picture of the Richard Long. I simplified the process by standing above and started snapping away moving along or down for each picture in a rough grid. Five rows of five. Twenty-five pictures in all. If I was to put all these photos together I would have an almost life-size replica of the Richard Long original.

I lifted the picture up and let it drop face down into a patch of thistle, put a new cartridge of film into the camera and started again. Five rows of five. (This felt good, like I was really making something.) Then the sun went in and the glorious grey returned.

I shook myself down, pulled myself together, loaded the frame into the back, climbed up onto the driver's seat, yanked out the *Bob Dylan's Greatest Hits* cassette, shoved it back down among the chip wrappers and used notebooks. I had a job to do. A man's job. I celebrated my regained sanity by sticking up a couple of placards on two forms of fellow advertising that surprised me in this otherwise baron landscape. 'Caithness Glass welcomes you to our county and factory at Wick' and 'Massed Pipe Bands, Riverside, Wick, 10th June 3.00 pm to 7.30 pm'.

Down through the hamlets of Reay and Isauld I rode, then up and around the bend and the end was in sight. In the grey drizzle of this perfect day I could see my long-lost cousin, the Dounreay nuclear power station.

'Cousin? What do you mean cousin?'

'I don't know. It just came out that way.'

For once I drove slowly. We had a childhood family holiday up there on that north coast. It was sometime in the mid-1960s, we were in our caravan. It rained all the time. It was a great holiday. I was able to spend most of my time fishing or wandering around up on the Flow. On this holiday we did a guided tour of the power station. It was shiny and modern; men — women, even — were wearing white coats. Nuclear power was the future. Endless clean energy, it would solve all the world's problems.

The first Sunday back after this holiday I remember my Dad preached a sermon about nuclear power. The basic theme was how power could be used to create evil ends or good deeds. It was down to us to choose, we were responsible. How we used or abused the little bits of power we had in our families or work places or as citizens of the world — Hiroshima or endless clean cheap energy to solve the world's problems. Of course things have changed since then. We no longer trust men in white coats. Maybe I should conduct an experiment, get myself a white coat to wear while writing to see if it makes what I write more believable.

But we still love nuclear power stations. They either provide employment for us if we live in far-flung, low-density corners of this island or they can act as icons, to focus all our conspiracy theory-driven paranoia about governments doing dastardly deeds in secret. Lobsters sprouting breasts and haddocks growing horns and things that glow green in the night sneaking into the food chain for Jamie Oliver to sell us while he does his adverts for a supermarket near you. Maybe he should try wearing a white coat.

As I said, I drove slowly. Was this out of respect for 1950s modernism or out of fear that the cctv camera would notice my tax disk was four months out of date and this little jape of mine would be crushed just as I was about to cross the finishing line?

I made my way around the perimeter fence, sticking up the placards wherever it felt appropriate and where I felt I wasn't being watched. 'Perimeter' and 'fence' are a couple of words that when used together always get us buzzing.

In my lifetime I can't recall a week going by without the phrase 'perimeter fence' getting into the news.

Does society need more or less perimeter fences? Would you like your own one? A mobile one you could carry around with you like a can of mace or a mobile phone, or would that just cause a rush on bolt cutters that the manufacturers could not supply?

Is the perimeter fence around Dounreay a more perfect example of the genre than the one around Stonehenge? Do perimeter fences contain more symbolic power than what they perimet? Should perimeter fences have preservation orders? Is anybody currently writing a book titled *The history of the perimeter fence?* Should I organise my own slide-show/talk tour 'Perimeter Fences I Have Loved'? Had Ross Sinclair done a picture of himself, top off, back to the camera, to reveal his 'REAL LIFE' tattoo, outside the Dounreay perimeter fence and called the picture *Real Life Admires a Perimeter Fence?* Ross Sinclair is an artist who goes around looking at things and having his picture taken, back to the camera, top off, revealing his 'REAL LIFE' tattoo. I like what he does, I don't know why.

I love perimeter fences because they make life more interesting. What would Steve McQueen have done if he hadn't had that perimeter fence to jump, in *The Great Escape* or the Greenham Common women if they hadn't had one to camp by? It's close-knit communities that you should be concerned about — every time the newsreader says 'close-knit community' you know people are being killed. My advice: never build a nuclear power station near a close-knit community if you don't want a disaster to happen.

The first placard I put up around the site is on a Vulcan Naval Reactor Test Establishment.

Wasn't Spock in *Star Trek* a Vulcan? Was this place anything to do with him?

As I made my way around the perimeter fence, with the giant

golf ball dome at the centre, I realised I was following some basic religious instinct. Like Muslims walking around the Ka'Ba or Joshua walking around the walls of Jericho with his 40,000 men? Or Gimpo driving around the M25? I even got to thinking that the sheep grazing within the perimeter fence were being bred for sacrificial purposes. I mean nobody would actually want to eat their roast lamb on a Sunday if they knew it had spent its life grazing within the perimeter fence of a nuclear power station.

One sign on the fence warned me about the danger of 275,000 volts and I wondered who had counted them all and what they looked like. Was it enough to light the light of this world and couldn't I have just one little touch?

The man at the gate told me there were no guided tours these days and I should follow the signs to the exhibition centre, half a mile down the road. The exhibition centre was a dismal affair. All big, blown-up photos of men at work and text giving us a brief story of how nuclear power was made. No pictures of lobsters with breasts or what leaking radiation looks like or even a picture of Hiroshima. The place was unmanned. My suspicions led me to believe that this was a safety precaution. If they had a friendly guide at the exhibition centre s/he might become the focus of unruly anti-nuclear protesters. I decided that I should put up one last placard on the outside of the exhibition centre. When I rummaged around the back of the Land Rover I found there were none left, other than the three that people had signed the back of. At least this resolved one problem that had been troubling me since day two of this drive up Britain. I could no longer be tempted to sneak back to stick up placards and take photos, then pretend they had been taken during those four days.

As I flick through the photos now I realise there are vast gaps left unrecorded of this trip but that's reality for you. You wouldn't want me doing any of that Richard Long jiggery-pokery with the photos. Since doing this drive up Britain and, inspired by David Hockney paintings of the EastYorkshire Wolds that he did in the mid 1990s, I've been reading some of his theories about photography being dead and how as a medium it could never be trusted in the first place and all that tyranny of the single-point perspective stuff. Maybe this is the excuse I need, to get back to painting. Do a few big canvases from my imagination of what I think the M180, the Humber Bridge, the M62 and the Forth Bridge would look like if I'd had time to put one of the placards on them. I could call the series 'An Artist's Impression of a Job Not Done' and, of course, I would use none of that single-point perspective tyranny and I wouldn't be lying. Or I could just do the one painting. A closely cropped portrait of a placard. It could stand as a symbol for all the places I missed. Unknown Soldieresque

I had had another idea of what to do with any excess placards, thus removing the temptation to sneak back. It was to scatter them on to the sea, as close to the nuclear reactor as I could get.

The placards would float off into the ocean, pick up a dose of radiation on the way, sail the seven seas and then get washed up on some far shore to be found by an art-collecting beachcomber with $20,000 to spend. The message in a bottle method of self-expression does not lose its romantic pull and anyway I could use it again some time as the central medium of communication for a brand new venture.

I was still left with the disappointment that I had no placard to stick on the exhibition centre.

So I took a picture of it anyway.

I then became aware that I was in need of a turn out, so I re-entered the visitors centre, followed the signs that led to the lavatories. There was a choice of two cubicles. I chose the one next to the wall. Wiped the seat with bog paper so as not to catch any germs from strangers. It was as I was sitting there reading the work of the previous bog-wall scribblers that I first thought that my memories of these past four days could be turned into a book. Of course I would have to run the risk of misquoting numerous people as I stuff words into their mouths for the sake of argument. If I proclaim it to be a work of fiction it might get me round their chagrin. As it turns out anything that is such a celebration of the highly subjective could not be viewed as anything less than fiction.

Taking the pencil from my pocket I wrote the word 'acknowledgements' on the wall. I then wrote a list of all the names of the people I could remember who had, in some way, been involved, supportive or inspirational in this excursion. Out of force of habit I took a snap of my handiwork, thinking I could use the picture in this proposed book. Undoubtedly I was being influenced by Paul Graham here. He had spent almost all of 1999 visiting every gentleman's public lavatory in the south-east of England, photographing the bog-wall scribbler's work. It sounds corny but his finished prints were works of exquisite beauty. I also planned to return, sometime soon, to the 'For Mum and Dad' graffiti and take a picture of that to use as well.

I wiped my arse, checking the bog paper for traces of blood. You know what it's like with piles, they always show up when you've been away from home for a few days.

Washed my hands thoroughly while making sure I didn't catch my reflection in the mirror.

Time to interrupt the flow of this story again. I'm back in Safeway's Coffee Shop, putting off straightening out the tenses.

When I got in last night and told Sallie about the incident with the member of staff here, she said, 'Serves you right. Any time you describe a woman in your writing you basically sum them up as if you consider them shaggable or not. You never say if you think they are intelligent or interesting.'

There is very little point in trying to argue with Sallie, she can always get the better of me. So I just told her I'd try to do better and left it at that.

And sadly the acknowledgements picture I had taken was so out of focus that it was of no practical use. So today, as in now, after I've finished my second mug of coffee in the Safeway Coffee Shop, I'm going to go to the in-store conveniences, choose the cubicle next to the wall and try again. I know it lacks the spontaneity of my first attempt but I do want to get the job properly done. And anyway, there are a few names that got missed off the first list and names I got wrong. End of reality break.

Next to the exhibition centre was a Portakabin selling refreshments. It was empty bar me and the woman serving. She was 50-something and welcoming, though the only hot food she had was a vegetable broth. I asked for a bowl with a roll, a cup of tea and a KitKat and then introduced myself. Her name was Margaret. She was as warm and friendly as her soup but she didn't sell postcards. I wanted to send postcards to family and friends. Nuclear-powered postcards. As I supped my soup I tried to focus my mind on what I should be doing next regarding selling *A Smell of Sulphur in the Wind.* Being up there in the Portakabin with Margaret, her soup and the 275,000 volts nearby made the notion of a pokey little art-world show down in London a bit of an anticlimax, so I wiped my bowl clean, broke open the KitKat and decided I would put an advert at the back of this book with my e-mail address and see what happens. While I was at it I might as well sell some carpets and tins of grey paint. Maybe I could do a book launch in Margaret's Portakabin.

There was something else, other than what to do about the gaps in the visual record of my drive up Britain, that had been worrying me. My sciatica had been playing up quite a bit and if it carried on like this the plan to walk across Iceland from top to bottom would be a physical impossibility, it would wear my crutches out.

Anyway what did all this walking crap prove? There will be plenty of time for that when the oil runs out. So before it does, I should fly to Akureyri (top of Iceland), commandeer an all-terrain vehicle and drive down the fucker, stop off at what's left of Richard Long's stone circle, do the business and get the job done and be back home by tea-time on Friday night. I mean, doesn't Richard Long have a family life? All this spending months away from home in Patagonia and the like.

I spew this cynicism, knowing fine well I can never get through a fortnight without pulling Richard Long's *Walking in Circles* book from my shelves and stealing a few moments dreaming over his photos of jobs done in far-off lands. It's as bad as the Bob Dylan business.

To stop my mind trying to construct further unattainable goals I got the prints out that Chad McCail had given me, the previous day, to have a good look at. As well as the Garden of Eden one, there were a dozen others, all the same size, landscape proportion, about 15 inches by 7 inches. They were on white card and the drawings looked like they had originally been done with a Pentel-type pen. Each print depicted a scene of innocent idealism. The people in the scenes had no facial features, this worked well and added to your empathy with their struggles. Under each scene was a quote:

> People build homes and grow food.
> Roads are dug up.
> School is not compulsory.
> Armour dissolves.
> Mercy is shown.
> Land is shared.
> People stop using things.
> Wounds are healed.
> Soldiers leave the Armed Forces.
> Obedience doesn't relieve pain.
> People have relaxing orgasms.
> Money is destroyed.

There was something in the knowing innocence of these prints that I liked a lot. Although Chad suffered from a mild form of post-modernism he knew these prints contained fundamental ideals we should not lose or at least that was my reading as I licked the crumbs of chocolate from the KitKat's inner silver wrapper. I then realised these 12 prints would make serviceable, if somewhat oversized, postcards. I turned them over, drew a little rectangle on the top right-hand corner of each of them to denote the stamp sticking space. Put a line down the middle to divide the address area from the 'Wish you were here' bit.

Then, at the bottom of the left-hand side in the tidiest hand I could manage, I wrote, 'This is an original print by the young Scottish artist Chad McCail. Within the next five years he will probably be a big name to be reckoned with in the international contemporary art world and this print will be worth a few quid.'

Then I made up a quote of my own to put at the top of the left-hand side. My quote went, 'All war will end when women cease to find men in uniforms attractive — discuss.'

As I was leaving I handed these dozen large-format postcards over to Margaret and asked her to give them out to the next 12 customers to visit her Portakabin. I also told her that the soup was great.

Then I drove home.

Epiphany on the Slip Road

And that should have been that. Job done. Write up my notes. Get the book made, put it out and wait for somebody to send me $20,000.

But on my drive home, which I proudly did in one 12-hour dash, only stopping once for coffee and diesel, I became vaguely aware that I was driving down a different country to the one I had driven up.

It was only when driving up the slip road of the M1's junction 14, the Milton Keynes turning, that this vague awareness crashed through the barriers I had put up to stop any more of my highly subjective theories taking over. What caused the epiphany can be easily pinpointed. It was a placard, fitted to the signpost, which told us that motorway restrictions no longer applied. This placard was different in every way possible to the 'For Sale' ones I had been putting up: it was portrait as opposed to landscape; it was not made from correx but was, in fact, a poster that had been pasted on to a board that then had been tied, using string, to the signpost; it was crammed with too much text to take in at one passing; and there were too many typefaces for my liking; and design-wise it was a mess. It is a type we see all over the country at the moment. What it advertised was an all-nighter, 9.00 pm to 6.00 am. The text was mainly taken up with a list of the 23 DJs and 18 MCs appearing. But the biggest billing was given to the definition of music that was to be featured: UK Garage.

I'm not a big fan of UK Garage, whether it's the underground type or the Craig David chart-topping variety, but I do like the placards. I like reading the lists of the stage names chosen by the DJs and MCs.

I pulled up. I still had one reel of film left, so I got out and tried to do a patchwork of the poster. This time it was considerably harder than when I had done the front and back of the Richard Long. I was working in the dark, only seeing the position of the poster for a fraction of a second each time the flash went off.

Throughout the drive from Southampton to Dounreay, I never once thought I was motoring up the UK. It was always Britain. Great Britain. In an instant I became aware that the UK was a completely different country altogether. I had driven down the UK.

I now realise that my drive up Britain is the last I will ever make.

That in doing this drive I was saying my farewell to all that was Great Britain. I was not only drawing a wiggly conceptual line of placards up the island, I was also drawing a line under it ever being Great Britain again.

I am not claiming any originality in my thinking; cultural commentators may have already observed and pronounced upon the perceived psychological difference that exists between what is GB and what is the UK. If they have, I've not read it. For me this is personal, as any revelation should be.

So, do you know what the official name of this country is? Well I didn't, or at least I had forgotten. Before starting to write this postscript I had to look it up — The United Kingdom of Great Britain and Northern Ireland.

On looking it up I also discovered that the concept of us being British is a comparatively recent one. It was those great reformers, the Victorians, who tried to bring us all together as one happy family. We were no longer to be the Irish, Scots, Welsh or English, but all British. They encouraged the Scots to think of themselves as living in North Britain and the Irish as living in West Britain and the poor Welsh had to content themselves with living in a bit of South Britain with their English masters and a poodle prince.

It was the Romans who had defined us British as a race apart. Being British had never existed before the Victorians as a way we perceived ourselves. This is further complicated by the knowledge that the British Isles exists as a geographical definition of a group of islands, separate from any political definitions. In the same way Great Britain exists as the geographical name for the largest of this group of islands. Complicated even further with having to put up with the same monarch from 1603 until the Irish partially escaped.

So Britannia was invented and designed to look like she was a major mover on some ancient and classical pantheon. With her Union Jack shield to protect us all from the slings and arrows of lesser races and, of course, making sure Britons could *never, never, never be slaves.*

Look after the pennies and the pounds will look after themselves. For all of my childhood those pennies jangled in my pockets, every one of them starring Britannia. Kings may come and queens may go but Britannia was always there, the constant. She was Mother to us all. That was until decimalisation in 1971 and then she was gone from our coppers. Ever since, Britain and being British has been on the retreat. The British Restaurant had disappeared first after the war, British Standard Whitworth forgotten, British Standard Time a bad experiment, the British Thermal Unit gone, British Home Stores made over into BHS.

We no longer have the 'best of British' or suffer from the 'British disease'.

I used to imagine that if we only fielded a British side in the World Cup, we would win it every time. With Dennis Law, Nobby Styles and George Best in the same side, how could we ever lose?

In the late 1960s, a saxophone player, Mike Evans, wrote a song called 'GB Blues' that he would perform with the poet/rockers, The Liverpool Scene. Seven years later, Johnny Rotten was berating us about 'Anarchy in the UK'. The retreat from all things British was well and truly on its way.

For many, that retreat was into our separate nationalisms and regionalities. Plaid Cymru and the SNP are natural bedfellows of this move. But so are the various republican and loyalist parties in Northern Ireland. It's obvious what the republicans are trying to escape from. But loyalists, wrapped up in their union flags, are doing the same thing, as they try and reinvent themselves as red-handed Ulstermen of old.

Even the English have been getting in on it, if somewhat belatedly with their rediscovery of the cross of St George and all that 'England expects' rubbish. We might make useless Europeans but we are becoming more multicultural. The ethnic diversity of our population creeps onwards and outwards, as our service industries take root and blossom on the ruins of our manufacturing past.

There is hardly a hamlet left without an Indian or Chinese take-away. More of our population's first language is Urdu than Geordie. So as our white population tries to retreat into the various nationalisms, where does that leave the others? Paul Ince wrapped in the flag of St George doesn't work, nor does Colin Jackson in the Welsh Dragon or Linford Christie draped in the Union Jack.

And, of course, they can't escape back to the sub-continent or the Caribbean or wherever it is their parents or grandparents came from. No, they are here on this island with the rest of us mongrel lot, where they belong.

My first memory of something called the UK existing was in a lesson at primary school. We were learning to write our addresses and the teacher told us to put the two letters — UK — on the last line. I knew I lived in Scotland, I knew that Scotland was part of Great Britain and there had been this thing called the British Empire where the sun never set. But this UK business was new to me. At the age of eight I thought it was something that only existed on letters and parcels. Nothing to do with what defined us as people. More the back end of a postcode than a place to have home thoughts from abroad about.

When Jimmy Cauty and I used to make records, a friend of ours called Tony Thorpe would drop by the studio to give us advice. Tony was blackness personified. There is not a man in all of Africa more black than Tony Thorpe. And it's not just his colour. He fitted all the other stereotypes: muscle bound, rhythm leaping from every pore and a big cock. Tony went on holiday to Jamaica to visit his granny. In Kingston they laughed at him for his English ways. The way he walked, the way he talked and the way he cut his hair. Obviously having a liking for goat curry and the complete works of Augustus Pablo was not enough.

Back in London, Tony was part of the generation that evolved the Jungle and Drum 'n' Bass musical genres of the early to mid 1990s. Tony said to me, 'Bill, this is the first time we have made our own music and not just tried to copy music from Jamaica or the US.' Tony was including Jimmy and me in the 'we.' I felt flattered so I refrained from saying, 'But Tony, we've been making our own music for 2000 years, from plain chant to heavy metal.' I knew what Tony meant — first and second generation blacks making music that didn't have to be a pale imitation of the real thing from Kingston or New York.

Of course neither Jungle nor Drum 'n' Bass ever crossed over from being specialist to mass market in the way that UK Garage has. Although garage was initially the term used to describe the music played at the Garage (Gay-Raj) Club in New York in the mid 1980s — soul divas doing their thing over stripped down backing tracks. What we now know as UK Garage owes very little to what got those black gays going 15 years ago in Manhattan.

UK Garage is truly the coming of age of black music created on these islands. And there is no way it would have ever been called GB Garage. It could be argued that this is only because UK sounds tougher, sexier, cooler than GB. Almost like a sportswear logo, not quite as good as Nike but certainly better than Adidas.

But it's not just being used by a bunch of black kids and all those wannabe ones. It's everywhere. As Great Britain recedes over the horizon along with the sun that never set, so the UK takes hold, emerging from the shadows. And this UK has nothing to do with the United Kingdom of 1603, 1707, 1803 or any other date in its history, and definitely not connected to any Europhobic political party, it's just those two letters that sound good together.

What could the French Connection clothes shops have done with the letters GB to advertise their wares?

I might have been able to spew a version of this rhetoric out at any time over the past ten years but it was only on seeing that poster at junction 14, the Milton Keynes turn-off, on that night after my voyage down this land that it hit me. I'm not Scottish or British or half English or South African. No, I'm none of these things. Those are descriptions that root you to a past, tie you down like Gulliver in Lilliput.

I am UK'n. Pronounce it like Canadian, Jamaican or Australian, Nigerian or even American, but being UK'n I can dispense with the vowels and just use an apostrophe. 'Ich bin ein UK'n' to JFK it.

These are some of the positive things about being a UK'n — we never covered the globe with pink, never won two World Wars or a

World Cup. We never traded in slaves or had just one mother tongue or the seas' most feared navy. We never had to pass Norman Tebbit's cricket test. Never had to bear allegiance to the Queen. Never had to worry if the beer was warm or wish we had a better national anthem. We weren't responsible for Brit Pop, Brit Art, Brit Lit. We don't know what the Dunkirk spirit is or what the British Legion is for. The 'we' is somewhat royal because maybe I'm the only UK'n there is. And, as I have no wish to be a leader and lack the missionary zeal, expect no call to arms, the clarion will be left unblown.

But I can tell you it's easy to be UK'n. It doesn't matter what colour, creed, sex you are. That includes Jews, Muslims and paedophiles. It doesn't matter where you come from, where you're going or how long you've been here and any or no passport will do. And all that Pound versus Euro stuff is irrelevant. You don't have to feel grateful to the fallen or guilty about your past. All it takes is a wish to live here on these islands with all the mess that's going on. As for being patriotic, no need to bother. There is nothing to be patriotic about, however much a scoundrel you are. This UK'n business for me is an ideology-free head zone. Even Al Fayad can be a UK'n.

The next thing I saw after seeing the poster for the all-nighter, was the chevron sign around the roundabout at the top of the slip road and I had an instant vision of a flag I wanted to hang on my wall.

If you have read other stuff I've written, you may know that I have loved the Union Jack. My love for it was inspired because it represented so many contradictions and has been appropriated by so many conflicting parties, causes and fashions. In that instant all my emotions were wiped clean to be replaced by a love for a flag that didn't, as yet, exist. This flag would have no red, white or blue. And there would be no room for the secondary colours of orange, green or purple. That just leaves yellow and black. A yellow chevron on a black background.

You might be thinking that flags are the last thing a UK'n should want. Flags are about tribalism, kings and queens, going to war. Well, no, 'The Old Chevron', as I now call it, is the opposite to that. Anybody else that wants to be a UK'n can design and make their own flag. I don't expect anybody to salute my one but me.

The next thing I noticed was a GB sticker on the car in front of me and I thought, 'I will get myself a UK sticker done.' Black lettering on a yellow oval background.

Then as I got around the roundabout, there was one of those signs pointing in the direction of some half-built estates of starter dream homes. You get them all over the place in Milton Keynes and I had a vision of how I could tie all the strands that have evolved over these past four days. I could take up David Jones' idea. Approach Wimpey or Bovis and get the loan of a show house for a month. In one room I could hang *A Smell Of Sulphur In The Wind.* Put a stack of 'For Sale' carpets on the floor. For sale at a thousand quid each. In another room will be all the photos I've taken as evidence, mounted in frames. One frame for each of the days. And Ray's Michelin Map, if he can loan it to me, to show the route I took. In another I will have the Penkiln Burn Tea Room (freshly baked cakes daily) and a 'Tea Room' carpet on the floor. The master bedroom can be stacked with a thousand tins of 'Drummond's International Grey' (each can a different shade). Another room will be given over to all things UK'n: flags, bumper stickers etc. Maybe even a computer in the box bedroom where you will be encouraged to make an addition to the Open Manifesto.

Of course there will be no point in doing this until this book has been out for a couple of months to give you time to know all about it.

I had always intended on calling the book *A Drive Up Britain* but that doesn't sound quite right now. Maybe it should be titled *Drawing A Line.* What do you think?

The End

A BURDEN SHARED

14 August 2001

2.32 am. I can't sleep. This is my present tense. Your present tense is whenever you read these lines at some unspecified point in my present tense's future.

This evening I read through the text of this book one last time in search of stray apostrophes before it goes off to the printer in China. A book like this is only commercially viable if cheap labour is used.

Would you have paid more for it?

I've been lying in bed trying to work out what it is about my tale that feels unresolved, letting my mind drift through from the back page to the opening line, from the selling of tins of grey paint back to when I first took the Richard Long out into the field and wondered what I had bought. From where I'm lying I can see its dark shape hanging on the wall, where I suppose it will hang on and off until it's sold.

I slip from under the cover. Lift the work from the wall. Make my way down the stairs. Lay it on the kitchen table and stare at the thing. So what happens when it's sold? Just another burden for another bastard with too much loose change and something to prove. There is a voice in my head: 'Bill, just cut it up into 20,000 tiny pieces and sell the bits at a dollar a throw. A burden shared…' I get a screwdriver, a steel metre rule, a set of Stabilo pens and my Stanley knife. Undo the brass screws. Lift out the glass. Remove *A Smell Of…*, and using masking tape, fix it fast to the tabletop. Then I get to work with the steel rule and pens, gridding the thing up. First into 20 equal sized rectangles using black ink. Each of these 20 spaces I grid into 10 equal sized rectangles using red ink. Each of these 200 spaces I grid into 10 equal sized rectangles using a yellow ink. And lastly I grid these 2,000 rectangles by 10 again using a pale blue ink. That makes 20,000 of the little fuckers. Get my camera and take some pictures of the thing. It's now just gone 4.30. First light is streaking the eastern sky and the birds have started up. Using the Stanley knife I cut out one of the tiny rectangles. Theoretically it measures 11.2 mm by 4.05 mm. I was going to keep it as a keepsake but since it's about the size of a tab of acid I swallow it. Flesh of Christ and all that.

I peel off the masking tape, put the frame back together, put my implements away. I stand back to look at my handiwork. I don't know if I like what I see. Shoddy, slipshod workmanship. Maybe I've made a big mistake. It might have been worth $20,000 a couple of hours ago, it certainly isn't now. Climb the stairs. Hang it back on the wall. Slip under the cover and wait.

The Epilogue

22 June 2006

And this is the epilogue to the paperback edition of this book. It's almost five years since I wrote *A Burden Shared* and a lot has happened. For a start, my domestic situation has changed, I no longer live in the same farmhouse looking across the Vale of Aylesbury. The view from my window as I make these notes is decidedly urban, and includes a sign put there by the London Borough of Hackney Parks Department which reads 'Welcome to Albion Parade'. A small parade of shops stocks all the essentials, no need for weekly trips to Tesco's or wherever anymore. The number 73 stops right outside the front door every six to eight minutes, a night bus every 30.

Welcome To Albion Parade sounds like the title of a book by George Orwell, or without the *Welcome To* a bit like a follow-up to *Vanity Fair* by William Thackeray. Maybe I will have to write it one day. But if I did, it would be about the Turkish greengrocer, the family that runs the Chinese takeaway, the young Kurdish barber, the bookie's and the woman in the tattoo parlour. Right now I want to concentrate on writing up what has happened to *A Smell Of Sulphur In The Wind* over these intervening years, how the thoughts and ideas contained within what I wrote back then have evolved.

I pick up the story about two hours after I left off in the last edition, when I slipped under the cover and waited. I didn't have to wait for more than ten seconds before sleep came. The next thing I was aware of was the voice of Sallie, my then partner, saying, 'What the fuck have you done now?'

Now Sallie had, and still has, a healthy cynicism about contemporary art in general and what I do in particular. Back then she never claimed to have any sort of working knowledge or interest in the machinations of the world of contemporary art. But she accepted that I had to go through this thing, this selling-the-*Richard-Long* thing, this whatever-it-was thing. But it seemed she thought that I had now taken it a tad too far. As I lay in my bed, eyes still shut and only half conscious, she was standing in front of a piece of art that, as far as she was concerned, had a nominal value of $20,000, or at least had done when she went to bed the evening before. But now, some hours later, it looked like it had been vandalised to a point where it was worthless.

On fully regaining consciousness I couldn't but agree. I had even forgotten to put the Perspex that protected the artwork back in the frame. Breakfast was eaten in silence. Sallie took the girls to school. I was left alone in the house to ponder my folly. I did what I always do in moments of crisis: start writing. You may have just read what I wrote that morning, *A Burden Shared.* I then emailed the text off to Cally, the book's designer, so that it would be included as the closing chapter.

What I did then — for no good reason other than I still had some nervous energy to burn off — was to take *A Smell Of Sulphur In The Wind* down from the bedroom wall, out of the house and into our sheep field. I banged a couple of nails into the lintel of the entrance of the sheep shed. Then, using a length of bailer twine, I hung it up and stood there looking at it in the morning sunshine. For a few moments I felt a modicum of pride in what I had done. In those few moments I took the camera from my pocket and took a picture of the work. It was when I was unhooking the bailer twine from the two nails that *A Smell Of Sulphur In The Wind* fell face down in the sheep shit.

Back in the kitchen, with the use of a knife and a damp cloth, I was able to remove all of the sheep shit and most of the staining. Over a mug of tea, I started to ponder the problem of where to find 20,000 people willing to spend a dollar (or its sterling or euro equivalent) on a fraction of this fast deteriorating piece of art. To sell it to one person would be comparatively easy. You didn't have to be a venture capitalist to know you'd be on to a winner.

Even in these modern electronic times books take some time to publish. Between emailing the final bit of text to Cally and the book coming out was almost a nine-month gap. The publication date for *How To Be An Artist* was late May 2002. A friend of mine, Chris Brook, was programming a small literary festival called *Text* for the Phoenix Arts Centre in Exeter, where he then worked. He contacted me, asked me if I wanted to do anything. I told him about the book and told him I could come down and do a talk about the story so far in the hope that I could flog some of the 1/20,000 fractions of *A Smell of Sulphur*.... He was up for me doing two one-hour talks in the gallery space. They would pay me a modest fee and put me up in a smart hotel. I agreed.

I hadn't got a clue what I was going to do or say. I had never got up in front of a paying audience before, people who were expecting something that would justify them not staying in to watch the telly or going down the pub.

In the fortnight running up to these two performances my panic started to build. To allay the panic I undertook a series of displacement activities. The first one was to get the Dansette Monarch record player that my mum had bought in early 1967. It was the first electronic record player that we had owned as a family. It was on this record player that I played the first seven-inch 45 that I had ever bought. It was *Strawberry Fields* by The Beatles. Since the day I bought it at the age of 13 it has always remained my favourite record. I will return to this theme of my all-time favourite record and its effect on me another time.

I had a track called *True To The Trail* that I had written and recorded in 1986, cut as a seven-inch 45. It was an instrumental country-rock toe-tapping sort of tune. It was originally the opening track on an LP that I had done back then called *The Man*. Ever since it was recorded I had considered *True To The Trail* to be my signature tune. Not that I had any need for one, but just in case. The plan had been to have it as an edition of one. The trouble was that the pressing plant insisted on sending me half-a-dozen test pressings (white labels). I couldn't bring myself to destroy the superfluous copies, so instead I had a Penkiln Burn Recordings label made up and glued to the A and B sides of the first of these six test pressings.

I wrote a text called *Two Paintings*, which I had printed as a pamphlet. After that I painted the two paintings. They were both landscape proportions and measured 1.91m x 1.35m.

Doing these two paintings proved to be a lot more difficult than I thought it would. For a start, the local art shop in Aylesbury did not have the size of canvas that I was after and had to get it from an art shop in London, so I did not get the paintings done on the same day as the text was written, as originally proposed. There was another compromise that I had to make concerning the paint that I used. The romantic notion of using oils and enjoying the aroma of linseed oil got dumped in favour of the much easier to use and faster to dry acrylics. Both paintings were done within the week. On the first were the words 'A Smell Of Sulphur In The Wind' painted in black on a white background; on the second the words 'A Smell Of Money Underground', also black on white.

Then I had 20,000 flyer size cards printed up. These I called warranty cards. On one side of the warranty card was the photo I had taken of *A Smell of Sulphur...* as it hung in the door of the sheep shed moments before it fell face down into the sheep shit. On the other side was a space to stick on the 1/20,000 piece of *A Smell Of...* for safekeeping, a place for me to make my signature as the seller and a place for the buyer to put his or her signature. There was also the following text:

> Bill Drummond warrants that attached to this card is a 1/20,000 fraction of the artwork *A Smell Of Sulphur In the Wind* by the artist Richard Long.
> Bill Drummond warrants that as long as stocks of these fragments are still for sale, their value will remain at $1.00 each; and that once all the 20,000 fragments have been sold, he will take the 20,000 dollar bills to Iceland in an oak box and bury it at the centre of the stone-circle featured in the photographic content of the original art work.
> The buyer is welcome to buy as many portions as they wish and will be contacted by e-mail when all 20,000 have been sold with the date when the box will be buried.
> The buyer will inform admin@penkiln-burn.com of any

changes in their e-mail address and will be kept informed of any new developments concerning this undertaking.
The buyer will be able to visit www.penkiln-burn.com in order to monitor the progress of sales and to view the exact location of their fragment using the given grid reference.
Good luck.

Next I took to John Jones, the picture framers, 50 of the photos that I had taken of the FOR SALE placards that had been stuck on lamp posts, telegraph poles and gates while driving up Britain. These were the bulk of the ones that I had used in the original hard back edition of this book. Twenty-five of the photos that were taken in England were mounted in one custom made frame. Twenty-five of the ones taken in Scotland were similarly mounted in an identical frame. Once the job was done they looked great. Proper stuff.

Some weeks later I took to John Jones the 50 photos I had taken of the *Richard Long* as it lay on the verge of the road at the top of Scotland. Twenty-five of the photos were of the front. The other 25 were of the back. I had originally hoped that I could montage them together so they would look like those photomontages that David Hockney made in the 1980s using his Polaroid camera. When I first got my prints back from Boots (I wasn't using a Polaroid) I discovered that they looked shit trying to montage them up like a Hockney. Instead of accepting failure I spaced all 25 an inch or so apart in five neat rows of five in the same proportions that the Scotland and England ones had been done. Once John Jones had done their job they looked even better than the first two frames. Real art.

I had also taken 18 photographs of all four sides of *A Smell Of Sulphur In The Wind*. When Cally saw them he told me that he thought the front and back photos were fine but those of the sides were meaningless. He's too polite to say this but the implication was that my head was too far up my own arse. I value Cally's opinion on most things and took his counsel on this too. What I didn't tell him was that I had already ordered four long narrow frames for these 18 photos to be mounted in. These four frames are still cluttering up a corner in my workshop.

I strapped the two paintings on to the top of the Land Rover and loaded it up with all the other stuff plus the gridded-up *A Smell Of Sulphur In The Wind.*

Then I drove down to Exeter. On each of the 40 to 50 chairs that had been put out for possible attendees was placed a copy of the *Two Paintings* pamphlet. That evening, as I sat in what had been allotted to me as a dressing room and the waiting audience may have been reading the pamphlet, I was gripped with fear. The pointlessness of what I was doing was all too obvious. There was a small window in this room; it opened on to a backstreet. I thought of all the many reasons why I should climb through it and run away. Forever. Never to be heard of again.

At twelve minutes past seven I picked up the record player and my toolbox. Walked into the gallery from the back of the room. Put the record player down on the floor in front of the audience in the middle of the space, opened the lid and plugged it in. Opened the toolbox. Took out the 'one' copy of *True To The Trail* that existed in the world and put it on. While it was playing I returned to the dressing room and brought back the two paintings. One I set up stage left on an easel and the other on an easel stage right. Then I made a few more trips back to the dressing room to get the other bits that I had driven down with. By the time that lot was done the record was beginning to fade. I took it off and put the record player to one side.

It was only then that I turned to the audience and acknowledged them. I smiled, a hard thing for me to do.

'Good evening, my name is Bill Drummond. I am here to tell you a story, seek your advice and make a sales pitch. The story I am about to tell takes us, sort of, from here' — I indicated the painting stage right, *A Smell Of Sulphur In The Wind,* 'to here' — I indicated the painting stage left, *A Smell Money Underground.* "It begins in 1970...'

I spent the next hour or so telling the story so far. At the end of this I pulled out the *Richard Long* and invited people to buy. The friend I mentioned earlier acted as the banker. Anybody willing to buy a bit gave him 75p, he then handed them a dollar and a warranty card.

Then they came over to me and handed me the dollar. I stuffed the dollar in my back pocket. They chose the bit they wanted and, using the Stanley knife taken from my toolbox, they cut it out and, using a Pritstick also from my toolbox, stuck it to their warranty card. We shook hands. The deal was done.

The whole thing was a ramshackle mess but it also seemed like a success and I was glad I hadn't climbed through that window never to be seen again.

The next morning while tucking into a breakfast of kipper and brown bread and butter, I mulled over the major and very glaring problems in what I was doing. The first of these problems was that I had sold 64 sections of *A Smell Of Sulphur In The Wind* the previous night. If I carried on at this rate, I would have to do 313 more talks like this to get them all flogged.

The second and far more major problem was that every sodding punter wanted the fraction of *A Smell Of Sulphur...* that they were going to invest in to be from the centre of the photographic element of the work. This is the bit that depicts the stone circle built by the hands of Richard Long. Some others wanted to buy the handwritten text that is below the photograph. There was no punter stupid enough to want to buy a piece of the white mounting card, and two-thirds of the total work was this blank white card. It didn't take much imagination to realise that if I continued doing these sales pitches in the way I had done the previous night, there would soon be nothing but pieces of blank white card left to sell, and however good my sales pitch was, I couldn't imagine anybody going for them.

After finishing the kipper with only one bone getting stuck in my throat, I headed around to the local WH Smith's, got a sheet of card, a blue pen and a red one and retired to a coffee shop. I cut up 100 small rectangles of the card, each one about a couple of centimetres square. Then, using the red pen, I numbered them 1 to 100. Next I cut up 200 more rectangles of about the same size and using the blue pen I wrote 1 to 200 on them.

I usually have a bundle of supermarket carriers stuffed into one of my pockets. I pulled out two of them. Into one went the red 1 to 100 bits of card, into the other, the blue 1 to 200.

That night when I did the performance I used the bits of card in these two bags to create a lottery system. The punters were asked to dip their hand into one bag and lift out a card with a number on it. And then do the same with the other bag. Then they had the co-ordinates across and down of their 1/20,000 piece of *A Smell of Sulphur…*, no room for arguing. It worked well.

Back home, a bloke I knew who was a cabinetmaker made me a box out of English oak to keep the *Richard Long* in. He did a great job. That said, it's well heavy and is now pretty knackered and needs constant repairing, but it does look good. Next, a woman who did dressmaking in the village, made me a couple of shoebags with drawstrings, one made from blue material, the other red. On the blue one was the word 'Down' on the red one 'Across'.

There were some oak off-cuts left over from making the box. These I had cut up into 300 1cm cubes. On 100 of them I wrote 1 to 100 in red indelible ink; on the other 200, 1 to 200 in blue indelible ink. The cubes went into their respective bags. This lot replaced the two Tesco bags and bits of numbered card.

Since that night back in Exeter, I have done my *How To Be An Artist* performance 77 times to date. In doing it this many times I have learnt how to get up in front of people and talk. Learnt how to hold their attention. Or at least learnt how to stop too many of them falling asleep as I drone on about me, myself and I. I've even learnt how to get the odd laugh. There has only been one epileptic fit and two nosebleeds. As yet no babies have been born. And I have attempted to wear the same shirt, trousers and boots for each show.

I've been learning, I suppose, what stage actors have to do. That is, although I am telling the same story each time, I've got to reach down into myself and tell it to that night's audience as though I have never told it before. Sometimes I have failed and I'm just on autopilot. Other times I embroider the story to the point that I'm downright lying just to make the point or get the laugh.

As well as the art-establishment places around the country where you might expect something like this to happen, I've gone into prisons, schools, drop-in centres and numerous 'un-art' places. Obviously this makes me feel good in a 'what a great bloke I am, taking what I'm doing out there for the unwashed and those who don't give a toss' way. At The Warren, a drop-in centre in Hull, I was performing one afternoon to a bunch of jobless, semi-homeless 'scum', half of whose priority for the day was getting the wedge together for their next fix. I would be in mid flight, giving it the meaning of everything when one of them would pipe up with, 'Excuse me. Do you mind me asking you something?'

'Fine. Ask away.'

'Do you have a fag?' or even more humiliating, 'What the fuck are you on about?'

In the prisons or young offenders' units I could hear myself patronising them by toughening up my Scottish accent and dropping a few more 'f' words into the performance, telling them how I got kicked out of school in the hope they might connect with me in some way. But what I was going on about was so far removed from the realities of their own lives I was probably no more than an eccentric distraction for an hour or so.

So far I have limited the performances to mainland Britain (England, Scotland and Wales). For me, much of it — 'it' being the process of all this — is about this island, exploring up and down the motorways and many A roads. I see it as an ongoing job with something of the romance of a struggling band in their Transit on an endless tour of one-night stands with their dreams of playing Shea Stadium still intact even though to friends and family and anyone else who cares to have an opinion it's obvious that whatever chances they might once have had are long gone.

By the beginning of 2004 I had basically covered all the major conurbations in the country except London, which I was trying my best to avoid. But I still hadn't sold more than 8000 bits.

Gimpo, who was insisting on walking across Iceland with me when the time came, was beginning to get concerned that we might be too old to do it by the time all the bits were sold. In the mornings my knee joints are getting stiffer and beginning to ache. Getting younger isn't an option.

Even before I had done those couple of performances down in Exeter, I knew I wanted it to work as an exhibition as well, even before I started thinking about the major art exhibition in a metropolitan gallery I mentioned for the third edition. An exhibition in proper galleries, all the big regional ones around this country of ours. The ones that would impress me if I knew someone who was having a show there. But definitely not in some snobby little London one, full of blokes in black... I will restrain myself before writing anything else I may regret at a later stage. I don't want to go biting any hands before they have even thought about feeding me. Rightly or wrongly, I wanted what I perceived as the validation that shows in these types of places brings you. I wanted to show the art tutors who never even noticed me enough to lose interest in me, that I meant something. I know it's pathetic but it's often these small things that can give a man the drive to get all the way to the Oval Office just to prove something to someone somewhere in their past life.

I'm going to tell you how I got these various galleries to put on this exhibition of mine. I mean, I had never put on an exhibition in my life, let alone in a major regional gallery. I had no track record. It's true that people may have known my name from other stuff but not as someone who puts things up on gallery walls for other people to look at.

It sort of happened like this. Peter and Julian who run the art bookshop at the Arnolfini in Bristol had been given the opportunity to stage events in one of the gallery spaces there. These events were to happen in the turnaround time between major shows, when the gallery would be empty for a few days. They were inviting various writers to come and do something that was more than just a reading from their latest book — maybe exhibit some photos that related to the book, discuss how they work with the audience — their remit seemed quite open. Peter and Julian contacted me, knowing I had this *How To Be An Artist* book coming out. I leapt at the chance. Told them what I wanted to do, and they seemed to be up for it. There was not that much money in it but I could keep the door money. They really engaged with the whole thing and it was a success, mainly down to the work put in by them and their staff.

After the show at the Arnolfini I approached other galleries around the country, set up meetings with them. Told them how I could do a short show in their turnaround time; that I didn't expect that much input from them; that I would turn up with all my stuff in the back of the trailer; put the show up myself; and take it down a week or so later, sweep the floor and clear off. I didn't expect a fee, all I wanted from them was to sell the tickets for the performances and to keep the ticket money to cover my costs. The fact that I had already done this at the Arnolfini made it look like I knew what I was doing and I could deliver. It seemed to work OK, and most of the places that took it on were very supportive and gave a lot more than I asked for.

The first gallery that I approached was the Centre for Contemporary Arts (CCA) in Glasgow. I drove all the way from my place in Buckinghamshire in the Land Rover, setting off at 5am, with *Smell Of Sulphur...* and a couple of my framed photograph pieces in the back. I arrived there just after 2pm. Had a ten-minute meeting with Vivienne Gaskin, the then director of performance on the pavement outside, hauling the Richard Long and the other frames out of the back of the Land Rover and on to the road to show her. She said 'Great!' and agreed a date. I loaded it all up again and headed south, getting back home in the early hours.

It was also in the Arnolfini that I had one of the worst moments of my life, not in a dumped-by-your-missus or death-in-the-family sort of way, more like a bruised ego way. The first edition of *How To Be...* had already been out for a couple of months. I never thought to reread it once it was out. But on this day in Bristol, when I was ripping out pages from a copy of the book to Blu Tack to the wall, I noticed that the last page of the book was missing. It was not only missing in the copy of the book that I was ripping pages from, it was missing in every copy available in the bookshop downstairs. I went berserk. Not externally you understand, I didn't throw things or shout at anyone. This was my fault, I accepted that. I should have proofread the book, obviously. So what I did then was write a text explaining the missing page and my reaction to finding it missing and, along with the words from the missing page, publish a pamphlet. The pamphlets were sent to the book distributors, with instructions to put a pamphlet in every copy of the book leaving the building heading for a bookshop.

In this new edition of the book the missing page has been reinstated. But if perchance you are one of the people who bought the original edition and now you are reading this one — unlikely I know — and there was not a pamphlet entitled *The Last Page* inserted into yours, I apologise unreservedly.

The idea of what would be in this exhibition began with what I'd put together for the show in Exeter, as I've already described. But every time I had a chance to exhibit, it grew and it became more wordy, more bloated. I wanted the exhibition to tell the story, celebrate the process but mainly to look, well impressive, as if I knew what I was on about. I wasn't happy until every bit of wall space was covered and even then I wasn't happy. I exaggerate of course for the sake of word play but you get the picture.

At its most bloated the exhibition consisted of seven text-based posters, all the same size in identical frames. Seven text paintings, all the same size. At least 20 pages ripped from the *How To Be An Artist* book Blu-Tacked to the wall. I was so desperate to find novel ways of presenting the printed word that I bought one of those Dymo things that kids use to make labels and I started churning out texts with it. Then I would mount the Dymo text and have it shoved into a small but stout frame. There was also one of the large Richard Billingham photos that I had bought, one of the ones of his mother, which made him famous at the time of the Sensation exhibition at the National Gallery. There were assorted motorway signs. A Michelin metal map of Great Britain, the type you see on the outside wall of petrol stations next to the Michelin tyre pressure gauge chart, I had not been able to get Ray's one, so had to steal one from somewhere else.

Both the style and size of the text paintings and the posters that were developed for this exhibition have become almost a fixture in the way that I have been working in the past few years. There have been more than 25 of the paintings and 100 of the posters, each used in the various jobs that I have been working on. In a way the paintings have taken on a life of their own, which I have written about at length elsewhere.

At one end of the gallery space would always be the *Richard Long* lying in its oak box on a table. It was like an altarpiece. After the gallery visitor had read everything they were supposed to have read, they could come over and look at it. Touch it. Smell it. Marvel at the way that it was falling apart. They could go through the process of buying a piece. They could then put their name, email address, the co-ordinates of the piece they had bought and the date in the book that I had made for everybody to do this. As well as documenting something for me to look at and think 'Look at all these people who are into what I am doing', I can use the information there to email every one of them once I've sold the lot and am off to Iceland to bury the money.

Then after they have done the book thing they were invited to take part in a painting-by-numbers exercise. This is done on an identical-size canvas to those I have been using for the aforementioned text paintings, measuring 1.91m x 1.35m. I drew on it with a pencil the outline of the letters S, O, L and D (in large Trade Gothic Bold Condensed for those of you who take an interest in typeface), then I gridded the canvas up in the way that I had done with *A Smell Of Sulphur In The Wind,* 100 across and 200 down making 20,000 rectangles altogether. What I required of the punter was, with the help of the numbers across the top and down the side of the canvas, to find the small rectangle of canvas that has the same co-ordinates as the piece of the Richard Long they had bought. On hand were two paint brushes and two pots of acrylic paint, one black, the other yellow. If their rectangle fell within the outlines of the letters, they paint it yellow; if not, black.

As *A Smell Of Sulphur In The Wind* disappears this painting grows. And the word SOLD becomes...well you know, that's kind of obvious. One artwork appears as the other is disintegrating. At one of the talks someone once asked what I was going to do with the painting when it had all been filled in by the 20,000 artists who had been part of making it. I didn't know. As far as I was concerned, it only worked as a work of art as long as it was still in the process of being filled in;

once it had been done it was redundant. My colleague John Hirst has suggested I should use it to bundle up the $20,000 when it is buried in the middle of Iceland. This seems like a more practical idea than the one that involves me lugging a solid oak box containing the dollar bills. Things change, ideas evolve and 'Oh that's the way, uh-huh uh-huh, I like it, uh-huh uh-huh,' to quote KC and his Sunshine Band.

I got a bit carried away with putting stuff together that could go into frames and be hung on walls. This was all done in an attempt to make it look like a proper art exhibition on white walls and everything. I think I was getting quite desperate to prove that I was for real. A real artist, one who worked hard and did things that weren't just perceived as stunts for the national media.

For some gallery visitors the exhibition told the story. That was if the gallery visitor was diligent enough or had an empty enough day to spend at least an hour looking at and reading everything in the gallery. But galleries aren't places to go and read things, that's what books and libraries are for. Galleries are there to go and look and see things. Obvious. An art tutor of mine spent a whole morning trying to explain and demonstrate to us the difference between looking and seeing. I don't remember what he taught us.

Most people at the Arnolfini, where the exhibition was first up, would walk into this space, have a quick glance about, see all this stuff to read and walk out again. Some would read a bit of one poster then go over to another wall and read a bit from one of the pages of the book Blu Tacked to the wall. If I was in the gallery manning the cutting up and selling of the *Richard Long*, I would have to resist the urge to grab them by the shoulders, shove them in front of the *I Have* poster and tell them 'Read this first and then work your way around the gallery.' I never did it.

I guess most people want an instant hit when looking at art. The whole reason for visual art is that it bypasses explanation. It plugs straight into the senses. And what I was doing in these gallery spaces was all about explanation. Even right now, as I write these words I am layering explanation on the explanation that already exists. But the truth is I like it. I love it. It's not just what the words are telling you, what they mean, I love the look of words too. I loved the look of these gallery spaces filled with words. Of course I wanted them mounted and framed, painted and stitched, branded and etched. I wanted the words to look good — to have visual impact.

A friend of mine, David Balfe, who has a big interest in film (not films, note) has been talking to me of late about how film works as a medium. Filmmakers have to show the story and not tell it. 'Show don't tell, remember that, Bill.' I understood what he meant. However well delivered the lines in a film by an actor, they are always second best to the actor being able to put over their emotions and the story just by their mere presence. The trouble is I love words, the more the better. I love Damien Hirst's titles for his artworks. Take those titles away and I would not be that bothered about the visual stuff that is left standing in the gallery. Take away *The Physical Impossibility Of Death In the Mind Of Someone Living* and all you have left is a dead fish.

The exhibition carried on growing, becoming more layered, every offshoot of the work being given space.

John Hirst, who I first met at Hull Time-Based Arts when I did a number of performances around Humberside, had started working with me on putting on these shows, as had Gimpo when he got out of prison in late 2002. We started making films as we went along because Gimpo had a high-quality video camera. These films also became part of the exhibition. There was one film of my hand cutting up 100 bits of the Richard Long while the show was at Cornerhouse in Manchester. There was another of 100 different hands painting in their rectangles in Lincoln. Then there was the big one, or at least the long one — way over two hours if not quite Andy Warholian in length. When I had done the original drive up Britain sticking up Correx placards and doing my sales pitches, I had not got a single placard up along the sides of the M62, the motorway that straddles this island from Hull in the east to Liverpool in the west. It also holds more than a special place in my imagination. In the past I've written about this special place at length, even used it as the inspiration for making a pop record (*It's Grim Up North* by The Justified Ancients Of Mu Mu, 1991). Now I wanted to make the film. I made one of the text paintings. Visually, it was a total replica of one of the original 500 Correx placards.

We — that is, Gimpo, his brother, John Hirst and I — drove to Hull. Strapped the painting to the left side of the Land Rover. Then Hirst and myself started driving along the M62 in the middle lane. Gimpo's brother drove his car next to us in the inside lane, both of us going at a steady 50mph. Gimpo filmed the painting on the side of the Land Rover for the two hours and twenty minutes it took us to get to Liverpool.

The film is an epic of minimalism. We had set off very early in the morning as the sun was rising, its rays hitting the red, white and red bands of the painting and bouncing back deep into the lenses of Gimpo's camera. There was plenty of dangerous driving and plenty of truck drivers totally pissed off with us hogging the middle and inside lanes.

Gimpo had mic'd up the inside of the Land Rover. Whatever sound the mic recorded was to be the soundtrack. This turned out to be, at various times along the route, the Today programme on Radio 4, *Tigermilk* by Belle And Sebastian on the tape machine and me singing along with the sound of the engine.

I've written about what comes next earlier this year. What I wrote then may be published as part of a book that I am working on to be called *17*. That book will not be published until late 2007 or even 2008. It will be a book about music and this imaginary choir that has existed inside my head for some years now. The choir is called The17

Since I quit making pop records in 1992 plenty of people have asked me if I was ever going to return to making music. I always said 'No!' and I meant it. After three or four years of saying this in no uncertain terms, I realised I was lying. Most of my life I have been drawn to the sound of choral music of all sorts from any part of the world. The weird thing is I have never been drawn to actually wanting to buy recordings of choral music or even go to concerts of choral music but if I heard it by accident, it would speak to me in away that no other music did. If I was to think about it and give some rational explanation for this, it would be to do with the fact that in choral music something of the collective soul of mankind is being expressed as opposed to the individual ego of a solo singer. This choral music could be anything from Bach's St Matthew's Passion to those women in Bulgaria, from some tribal stuff in New Guinea to the Red Army Choir. I began to harbour fantasies that once over the age of 60 enough time might have lapsed between when I was 39 and quit pop music for me to try my hand at composing choral music without it looking like 'ex-pop star blah, blah, blah'. Everybody would have forgotten about me or at least my involvement with pop, so I would escape the accusations of dilettantism and trading on my past chart success.

Whatever. Being 60 was a long way off, I had plenty of time to fantasise about what these future choral masterpieces would sound like. Most of these fantasies occurred while I was driving alone in the Land Rover. It was the deep sound of the diesel engine, the wind whistling through the wing mirror, the roar of the overtaking trucks and the 101 rattles that the machine makes, which fired and inspired these fantasies. This music sounded primeval and wild. Unconstrained by mere melody and rhythm.

The film soundtrack was crap compared to what I thought the film looked like in all its 'minimal grandeur'. I might have just turned 50 but it was time to make my first choral masterpiece.

A couple of months after finishing the drive along the M62 I drove back to Hull with Kev Reverb, one of the great inspirational musicians of his generation. Kev also runs a small recording studio in Leicester called Memphis, where I go if I ever feel the need to try something that requires sound recording. In Hull, Reverb mic'd up the Land Rover, plate mics on the floor to capture the bass throb, another couple hanging off the mirror to capture the other frequencies. We drove along the M62 at the same speed as I did when filming and did it within a couple of minutes of the first drive.

On a few days over the next few weeks Reverb and myself worked with what amounted to 17 singers, building up and sculpting the choral soundtrack to the film. These singers were not proper classically trained singers but the blokes in any of the local Leicester bands that were using his studio at the time.

The process of doing this choral soundtrack not only unblocked my resistance to making music, it fired me up and I was overcome and overflowing with all sorts of ideas for what music could be about and what The17 should sound like. I wrote the following statement that now hangs as a framed poster in Kev Reverb's studio in Leicester.

> All recorded music has run its course.
> It has all been consumed, traded, downloaded,
> Understood, heard before, sampled, learned,
> Revived, judged and found wanting.
> Dispense with all previous forms of music and
> Music making and start again.
> Year zero now.
> --
> The17 is a choir.
> Their music has no history, follows no traditions,
> Recognises no contemporaries.
> The17 has many voices.
> They use no libretto, lyrics or words; no time
> Signatures, rhythm or beats; and have no knowledge
> Of melody, counterpoint or harmony.
> The17 struggle with the dark
> And respond to the light.

Then I decided the music we had recorded for the film was called *Drive* and I scored it so that others could perform it. This score is also printed on a poster. The score did not use musical notation, just words. It read as follows.

> Choose a journey.
> Record the sounds within your car or cab as you
> Drive your journey.
> If you are female find seventeen women willing to sing.
> If you are male find seventeen men willing to sing.
> Gather The17 together in a darkened room.
> Play them the recording of the journey.

Indicate a dominant note in the recording for them to pitch to.

Ask them to open their mouths and bring forth noise.

Ask them to listen and respond to the noises being produced by the other singers.

Use your initiative.

Now you will probably be able to tell from this that I'm pretty proud of this film and its soundtrack. The thing is, I have never shown it. Never even watched it myself. Feel no need. I don't expect anybody to sit and waste two hours and 20 minutes of their life watching a film of a painting strapped to the side of a Land Rover being driven from one end of the M62 to the other.

Since scoring *Drive* I have set about composing and scoring 16 other works for The17 to perform. I should add here that The17 is not a fixed choir. You can form your own version of The17 today. Each of the 17 scores are available at www.the17.org to download, including the classic *DECIDE* which I will not refrain from rewriting out here in the hope that you might perform it yourself when 21 November is next upon us.

No hymns will be sung.
No records will be played.
iPods will be left at home.
Rock bands will not rock.
Conductors will not take the podium.
Decks will not spin.
The needle will not drop.
The piano lid will not be lifted.
Films will have no soundtrack.
Jingles will not jangle.
Milkmen will not whistle.
Choirboys will shut their mouths.
Recording studios will not roll.
Mcs will not pass the mic.

Brass band practice will be postponed.
The strings will not serenade.
Plectrums will not pluck.
Record shops will be closed all day.
And you will not take part in any sort of music whatsoever.

Then you will decide what you want from music.

To be performed on No Music Day; 21st of November, every year.

Visit nomusicday.com and register the fact that you will be performing this SCORE.

The promotion of the *How To Be An Artist* exhibition and performance became part of the artwork itself, printing up fly-posters specifically for each town or city. Art galleries don't usually use fly-posters as a means of promotion. Fly-posting is seen as an ugly blight on the country's urban landscape. Local councils are at constant war with those who put up fly-posters. Local councils also provide large chunks of money for the type of regional art galleries I was showing in. This meant that I had to organise putting up these posters myself. What the posters did was inform a sizeable section of the public that would not normally be reached by the promotional techniques used by art galleries. In short, they worked and many of the people who bought tickets for the performances did so because they had seen the posters. The fly-posters were in the same style as all the posters I do. They would read something like this:

NOTICE

BILL DRUMMOND
WILL PERFORM
HOW TO BE AN ARTIST
AT CORNERHOUSE
MANCHESTER
ON THE 24, 25, 26, 29 APRIL
AND 1, 2, 3 MAY

AT 7PM
PLACES ARE LIMITED SO PLEASE BOOK EARLY
TICKETS FROM BOX OFFICE
£7, £5 FOR CONCESSIONS
OR BY TELEPHONE: 0161 200 1500
OR ONLINE: WWW.CORNERHOUSE.ORG

When I was to be doing *How To Be...* at Cornerhouse, the visual arts director of the place, Kathy Rae Huffman, was initially concerned that I wanted to do more than two performances at the gallery. In the past, she told me, artist talks, even when free, had never done well. The biggest audience that had ever turned up for one was for a talk given by Tracey Emin and even then they had only sold 35 of the 40 available tickets. I was proposing to do five shows and sell the tickets at considerably more than the £2 or £3 that artist's talk tickets usually go for. As far as I was concerned, what I was doing was far more than an artist mumbling about their work — it was part lecture, part performance and part entertainment and it cost me a load to put on. And I didn't want to be subsidised by anybody but those who were willing to pay for tickets.

A few days before the first show tickets sales were looking sluggish. It looked as if Kathy Rae Huffman was going to be right. Then the fly-posters went up around the centre of Manchester and all the shows sold out almost immediately. We added two more and, according to their box office people, they could have gone on selling out shows all month. So maybe this sounds arrogant, me bragging about my pulling power, but there is another reason for me wanting to stick this in here. If you are putting on an art show, don't just promote it to those that you already think would want to come, try and get the world at large to know about it.

For a time I was even photographing the fly-posters that had been put up and using five from each city, mounting and framing them and hanging these as part of the show. It was almost as if the exhibition was becoming an exhibition about itself. The navel gazing back at the eye.

At the same time that I started doing the fly-posters I made a painting almost identical to the one that was based on the *FOR SALE* placards and had been strapped to the side of the Land Rover for filming.

This one read:

BILL DRUMMOND
PERFORMS HOW TO BE AN ARTIST
CORNERHOUSE 24 APRIL – 3 MAY.

It hung in the gallery bar for a couple of weeks before the show with a framed poster beside it. The text on the poster read:

NOTICE

Buy a one twenty-thousandth fraction
of the photography and text work
A Smell Of Sulphur In The Wind
by the artist Richard Long for one U.S.
Dollar. Each fraction measures
Approximately 11.2mm x 4.05mm.
To know why where and how it is being
Sold read the book, visit the exhibition
Or attend the performance *How To Be An*
Artist.
Further Details at penkilnburn.com
Warning: A one twenty-thousandth fraction
Of the above-mentioned work may hold
no aesthetic or investment value.

At each of the subsequent exhibitions or performances of *How To Be An Artist* I have over-painted the venue and date information on the poster. This has now been done eight times. The paint on the canvas is now getting lumpier and thicker and more difficult to do each time. As with the SOLD painting, I like the fact that this painting serves an ongoing and almost practical purpose and once the last of the *How To Be An Artist* shows has been done, it will no longer have a purpose and will be ripe for the skip. Or if the spirit of recycling is upon me that particular day, I will reuse the canvas to start a brand new painting.

At the CCA in Glasgow, the one and only copy of *True To The Trail* got nicked. If you are the sod that nicked it, I hope your bad karma has come around and got you and your trail has been less than true. Personally I have always found it difficult to stay true to any trail. This is a case in point. I said this was supposed to be the only copy of this record in the world, so what do I do? I get one of the other five test pressing that I had not destroyed, have a couple more labels made up and now have myself a brand new one and only copy in the world.

At Cornerhouse, a member of the audience told me that he had seen a fraction of *A Smell of Sulphur…* stuck on one of the warranty cards for sale on eBay. It was being described as an original and signed work of art by Bill Drummond, and that the price had already reached £45. He wanted to know why I had given my word on the warranty card that the value of the thing would remain at $1 when here it was being flogged for more than 60 times its stated face value. And was I in on this? Who was scamming whom? I told him, and the rest of the audience, that I wasn't in on it.

Up until then most people would only buy one fraction or maybe a couple for friends. Nobody had bothered to buy serious multiples. That night numerous people were buying multiples of ten. Someone even asked for 50 of them. The next day there was plenty of eBay trade in signed original art works by Bill Drummond. I was heartened to see that the resale value soon came tumbling down.

Some time ago I read an interview with Damien Hirst. The market value of art was being discussed. I think Hirst was being called to account for the vast sums he was charging these days for his works. He claimed he never sold them for any more than they are worth. He was asked how he knew their worth. He answered, 'Whatever anybody is willing to pay for them.' Love it or loath it, the basic capitalism of the marketplace would determine the resale value of these bits of cardboard. I had no say in the matter.

But the value of art has for many years had a grip on the public imagination and it is something I have played with from time to time.

Here is one of the posters that appeared in the *How To Be An Artist* exhibition.

NOTICE

TO MAKE MONEY
BILL DRUMMOND HAS PRINTED MOST
OF THE PENKILN BURN POSTERS IN
EDITIONS OF ONE HUNDRED.
THESE POSTERS ARE NUMBERED
AND SIGNED.
NUMBERS ONE TO NINETY
COST TEN QUID.
NUMBERS NINETY TO NINETY NINE
COST ONE THOUSAND QUID
AND NUMBER ONE HUNDRED
COSTS TEN THOUSAND QUID.

This poster generated lots of interest and was the first to sell the 90 going at ten quid each. Nobody, to my face anyway, questioned the fact that I was selling a piece of paper with some print on it at 1000 times the price of another identical one. Another bloke at Cornerhouse came in and demanded to see the hundredth copy that was going to be sold for £10,000. I wasn't in the gallery at the time, I was in the office. John Hirst came through to me with an unnumbered and unsigned copy of the poster. I signed it and numbered it 100/100. He took it back through and showed it to the bloke. He asked if he could touch it.

In November 2006 I will be in Zurich giving a talk about money and its relationship to art. I guess they asked me over because of the more obvious stuff about money in my past work. I'd rather move on from that or at least dodge the issue for the time being. I won't be referring to it in my talk. What I will be doing instead is premiering one of my new paintings. The colours used in the painting are red, yellow, blue and white. The text on the painting reads:

FOR SALE
PENKILN BURN PAINTINGS
10,000 QUID EACH

My idea is that I will paint copies of any of the Penkiln Burn paintings that I have done for the sum stated above. The paintings will not be signed or numbered. I don't expect trade to be brisk. I will paint as many of any of these paintings that there is a demand for. There will be no limited editions and I will never sell them for more or less than the £10,000, whatever happens with inflation or my worth in the art market. Obviously there is nothing to stop anybody painting an identical one to the ones that I do. There will probably be a short manual on how to do that with each painting sold and text available at penkiln-burn.com.

If this writing about value comes over sounding smug, so be it. I will be the one looking like a mug if I don't sell any of these paintings. And I will also refrain from going on any more about 'money and its relationship to art'; maybe another place and time.

By the time the *How To Be An Artist* show got to the Leeds City Art Gallery in October 2003 the Open Manifesto, that had first presented itself as an idea to me while starring at a lump of Blu Tack stuck to my dashboard in 2000, was becoming a reality. So to add to all the other stuff with which I was cluttering up the exhibition was a text painting with the word 'OPEN', white out of blue. Hanging next to the painting, a framed poster read:

NOTICE

The Open Manifesto exists.
It exists to define what art is and what art is not.
And how art should be made.
And what art is to be used for.
And how art can be discussed.
And what there is to be learnt.
And whom it is for.

It accepts: Whatever is said today makes redundant what was said yesterday.

What was said ten years ago might be suddenly as fresh as what will be said tomorrow morning.

The Open Manifesto will never close.

The Open Manifesto needs more.

All new doctrines, dogmas or principles are welcomed for consideration to be added to the Open Manifesto.

WARNINGS: No jokers, no timewasters. Mean what you say even if you fall short of what you proclaim.

The site itself was not up until early 2004 and has been progressing in its own way since then. Please visit and contribute if you have anything worth adding.

It was also while I was in Leeds that I got asked by the journalist Warren Jackson to do a sketch and a few hundred words that somehow related to the sketch for his new magazine *Carlos*. What follows is the text that I wrote for *Carlos*.

> PUBLICITY STUNT
> November 2003
>
> Do you ever think about what the perfect publicity stunt would be to alert the population of the world to a particular brand or cause? I don't, or at least I try not to. A number of things that I have been involved with in the past have been described by individuals and the media as publicity stunts. I've hated this, recoiled with hurt pride. The shimmering beauty and artistic integrity of whatever murky activity I had been up to sidelined, denigrated, written off as a mere publicity stunt, thus stripping it of any...well, whatever my ego hoped it contained.
>
> I've learnt my lesson. I've decided that in the future whatever I do should exist outside the context of the mass media. That it should exist on its own terms and have no need of the

media for it to exert whatever power, passion or beauty it may have. A contradiction in terms maybe — I mean, I'm only communicating these thoughts because you are reading these words in this rarefied corner of the publishing world.

At the time of writing, I'm in Leeds. My 'How How To Be An Artist' exhibition has just opened here at the Leeds City Art Gallery. It is a prestigious regional gallery and I'm pleased with the way it looks. Tonight I'm doing the first of six spoken-word performance things that I do, also called 'How To Be An Artist', in the gallery space. I choose never to do these performances to more than 50 people. I like to keep it intimate. I've done this exhibition and live performance at a number of other regional cities. All the performances, bar one, have sold out.

It's 11.36am right now and just before I came out to start writing these notes I was told they had only sold six tickets for tonight's performance. I didn't dare ask how the other nights were selling. Of course, I've already worked out where the blame should lie. Only one of the local media interviews that I gave has run, and of the 300 posters that should have been fly-posted around the city centre and the universities, I've only seen three up. So it's nothing to do with me and my pulling power. But six fuckin' tickets, this is going to take intimacy to new levels. Maybe I should suggest we just go down to the pub, and for the price of a pint I will tell them my tale there.

What I need now is a hard-core publicity stunt. Something that makes the front page of today's Yorkshire Evening Post, something that gets people thinking 'That Bill Drummond, I've always dug his radical-maverick, fuck-the-system chic thing, I'd better get a ticket for one of the performances he's doing in town before they all sell out.'

On my way from the gallery to the café, where I'm writing these notes, my mobile rang. It was Warren Jackson from this magazine. He wanted to know if I had done the drawing and text for the next issue that I had promised. 'No, sorry Warren, but look do you mind if I don't do the drawings of the carpets we talked about but a drawing of a tin of Drummond's International Grey instead?'

'What's that?'

'It's this grey emulsion paint that I'm producing and promoting. "A different shade in every tin." I've just done this poster to advertise it, where I request the public uses it to paint any institution or object they find either morally or aesthetically offensive.'

And as I am saying these words into the mobile phone, I'm walking by the bronze reclining woman Henry Moore statue that is reclining outside the Leeds City Art Gallery. Henry Moore was from Leeds. When I first went to art school, Henry Moore was still considered to be Britain's only international art superstar. Of course I thought he was a load of bollocks and, even worse, he was boring, without emotional or intellectual depth. Nowadays I don't give a fuck about Henry Moore, don't think about his work from one decade to the next. Does anybody? That was until I went past the statue 30-odd minutes ago and had an idea.

This is the idea. I could get a couple of tins of Drummond's International Grey from the back of my Land Rover, give the reclining woman the once-over, then paste up one of the posters advertising the paint on its plinth. Then phone in an anonymous message to the news desk of the *Yorkshire Evening Post*. That should do it, secure the front page of that day's paper and sell all the unsold tickets for that evening's performance.

I cut short my conversation with Warren Jackson, telling him I'd be getting back to him later. Then I phoned John Hirst, who's working with me on the show.

'Hi John, I've got this idea that should sell the tickets.'

And I told him what I planned.

'Don't be fucking stupid, Bill. If you do that, all it will achieve is to confirm the suspicions of all those that think you have a chip on your shoulder about the art establishment, that what you do has no more to it than the publicity that it generates. And anyway the gallery would kick you out. Just go and get done whatever you are supposed to do for that *Carlos* magazine and deal with the fact that only six people in the whole of Leeds wanted to spend money on hearing what you have to say about anything.'

'Okay, John.'

Post Script (written 13 days later)
My ego would like it to be known that although that Monday did not completely sell out, all the other five performances did. And that although the reclining woman was left ungreyed, I'm still looking forward to finding the perfect morally or aesthetically offensive target.

Putting the *Publicity Stunt* story into this text has reminded me that I've not told you how I had 1000 tins of Drummond's International Grey made up with a different shade in every tin. But first, this is the text on the poster referred to in *Publicity Stunt*:

NOTICE

Drummond's International Grey is a brand of emulsion paint.
Every tin contains 1 litre of paint.
Every tin contains a different shade of grey.
Every tin is one of an unlimited edition.
Drummond's International Grey can be used for your own domestic needs
Or
Drummond's International Grey can be used in the public arena to paint grey any object or institution that you find morally or aesthetically offensive.

Please send documentation of your painting to grey@penkiln-burn.com
If your local stockist has sold out of *Drummond's International Grey* order direct from shop@penkiln-burn.com

The logistics of getting 1000 tins of paint with a different shade of grey in every one was a lot more difficult than I thought it would be. The only paint manufacturer we found that would agree to do the job was not able to put the labels on the cans. In the majority of tins of paint these days the label is printed directly on to the metal, not on paper that is wrapped and then glued around the tin. To do this direct on to the metal thing, we would have had to be ordering tens of thousands of tins of the stuff and not just a measly 1000. This meant we had to have the 1000 tins of paint delivered and 1000 labels printed separately. Then two colleagues, Keith and Stella, had to stick a few hundred of the labels on to the tins. This was all being done in time for the exhibition at the Arnolfini, back in 2002.

The 1000 tins of paint were then transported in a truck from Suffolk where the paint had been manufactured and the labels stuck on, down to the Arnolfini. The driver then loaded the lot out the back of the truck on to the quayside street outside the gallery. It was pissing down with rain, the labels were going soggy and in our rush to try to get all the tins into the dry, one of the pallets supporting a couple of hundred cans toppled. Lids came off. Drummond's International Grey went everywhere on the cobbled street. The traffic warden called the police. The police wanted to know what it was about. Someone took delight in reading out to him the NOTICE that relates to what you are supposed to do with this paint. The policeman then wanted to know what immediate action I was going to take to clear up the mess and let the traffic flow once more. What I wanted to do, but did not suggest to the officer, was push all 1000 tins of the paint off the quayside into the water and be done. This was all beginning to remind me of another thing that I had been involved with a few years earlier outside the House of Parliament on Christmas Eve and a few thousand cans of Tennant's Super.

The plan had been that the 1000 tins of paint were going to be exhibited as a 10 x 10 x 10 cube (almost) in the gallery, along with the poster and a brand new text painting that I had just done, one that I thought was the best yet. The text on the painting read:

FOR SALE
DRUMMOND'S INTERNATIONAL GREY
A DIFFERENT SHADE IN EVERY TIN
25 QUID

The paint, poster and painting were not exhibited. Another truck had to be hired to deliver all the cans to my workshop, where they have stayed ever since. I try to ignore them, but they sit there as a lasting testament to my many, and counting, follies. That said, I still love the idea of the paint's existence and hope one day to give it a public profile. I bet it was never like this when Yves Klein was getting his blue off the ground.

There was something else that you will have read about earlier in the book which found its inspiration in the original drive up Britain that I did, or to be more correct in the drive down the UK. It's the whole UK'n thing. I had the flags made up, five of them. They looked fantastic. For a few weeks I thought it looked like the best flag in the world, even better than the one that Libya has which is just green, nothing else. Even had the UK stickers made for the back of your vehicle to be used when motoring abroad. Then I realised that the whole idea would be confused too easily with the UK Independence Party and that type of reactionary thinking. I guessed that I would have to spend all my time trying to explain why it was totally the opposite to anything like that, so it got knocked on the head. I still think the flag is great.

I took out a full-page advert in the April 2003 edition of *Art Monthly*. It followed the form of most of the posters that I do. It had the word NOTICE big and bold across the top. Under that it said BILL DRUMMOND IS DRIVING. And under that in three columns it listed 48 cities, towns and villages across the length and breadth of Britain where I was to deliver the *How To Be An Artist* roadshow. And underneath the three columns was some sort of explanation. I was determined to cover every region in the country. I was on a mission. But what I was proselytising I was none too sure.

Of course there was still the practical need to get out there and flog the 20,000 bleeders.

But it turned out it was a lot more difficult than I thought to go everywhere with the show. If it had been shown in Leeds, galleries didn't want it in Sheffield. If it was going to be in Norwich, the gallery in Ipswich would pass on it. Not because they didn't think it was any good or that it wouldn't pull in punters but because they wanted to be seen to be the only gallery in the region getting it. They didn't want second-hand goods. I tried to push the point that the people in Ipswich who might be interested in coming along would not be put off because it had already been seen in Norwich. But that is not how it works and I had to accept it.

I had been looking for an excuse to get an Ifor Williams trailer. You will have seen loads of Ifor Williams trailers, even if you don't know you have. They are farmers' first choice in trailers, all over the country. I got one that could be pulled by the Land Rover, big enough to stand up in. I had three museum-standard crates made for the trailer. In them I keep all the stuff that is hung on the gallery walls. I was self-contained. Go anywhere at a moment's notice. The more off-beat the better. Have art, will travel. Give me an audience of no more than 50 people and I will talk for almost two hours. That includes a 15-minute fag, piss and drink break.

There was a new place in Bedford which wanted to have me on. It is called Bedford Contemporary Arts (BCA). They would only have me if they had me before Milton Keynes Gallery (MK G). The gallery space at the BCA was exceedingly compact compared with the acres of white walls I was getting used to. But I liked it and agreed to do the show in April/May 2004. My natural instinct was to cram as much as I could into the space. Sarah Bloomfield, the director of the place, had other ideas. Up until then, John Hirst, Gimpo and I would arrive to wherever the show was to be hung and make all the decisions about what would go where in the gallery space. This Sarah Bloomfield had other ideas.

As far as she was concerned most of the stuff we had turned up with in the Ifor Williams was superfluous to what the show was about.

'But I think that all this stuff looks good.'
'Well, you can hang it in your front room but not in my gallery.'

And she was right. Almost three quarters of the exhibition went back into the trailer and what was left on the walls made far more sense, was far more to the point. I have always understood the 'less is more' principal in theory but it seemed I had to go through the 'more is more' bit to have confidence in my own 'less is more' position.

Spring 2005 at Baltic in Gateshead, up in the north-east of England, they were running a series, billed as performance lectures. I was invited up by an organisation called Amino to do *How To Be An Artist* as one of them. It was to be in Baltic's main live art/lecture space, which holds 250 people. I was concerned.

Not wanting to do whatever I was doing to any more than 50 people meant that I could keep it relatively intimate. There was no need for a microphone, no PowerPoint technology. I could hold up one of the frames with 25 photographs in it and everyone in the audience could see it. I could see the colour of everybody's eyes. There was also another very practical reason for limiting the audience to 50: the whole cutting up and selling off process after the talk. If all 50 people wanted to buy, and many wanted to buy more than one, the process could take well over an hour. If there was no bar or other distraction in the space, it was a bit much to expect people to hang around for up to an hour to buy their bit.

I agreed to do the thing at Baltic. I did it and it worked. Even though I didn't use a mic and the bar was closed. But there was another problem in doing it in a larger venue — in order to project myself to this many people, I was becoming more of a caricature of myself, more of a showman. All my gestures were getting more exaggerated so as to reach the back row. I felt like I was becoming more like Billy Graham than an artist talking about his work to a few interested parties.

Another concern had been creeping up on me. In all the other areas of my practice I was trying to develop a way of working where the final focus of what I was wanting people to respond to was not about me. My ideal was that people would come across what I do and respond to it and engage with it without even knowing it was the work of an artist, let alone one named Bill Drummond. The *How To Be An Artist* performance was all about me. It was, and still is, all about me going 'Look at me and my over-convoluted relationship with a work of art.' I might try to convince you at times that it is really about everyone's relationship with art in these modern times, but I don't know if that washes even with me, let alone you.

Most of the time I wish I could dump the whole job and just get on with the other stuff that I have been doing, that I find more...well, more in keeping with what I think art should be about in these times. Something where the focus is not on me. Something that I want to do when I get up in the morning. I reckon if I had not done this whole *How To Be An Artist* thing myself and came across it being done by someone else, I would have hated it.

Then there is that old problem of the familiar taunt 'It has all been done before', that seems to haunt anyone involved with the creative process. When I started out on this cutting up and selling off process, numerous folks who knew their history of art took some delight in telling me about how, back in the '50s, Robert Rauschenberg bought a Willem de Kooning pencil drawing and rubbed it out using a rubber at the other end of a pencil and then exhibited the work retitled *Erased de Kooning*. If I had known about this, maybe I would never have started cutting up and selling off my Richard Long. This concerned me. Then when Jake and Dinos Chapman hit the national headlines for buying some Goya etchings and drawing funny faces on the figures that Goya had etched, I again questioned what I was doing and the way that I was doing it. But the worst was when Michael Landy did his *Break Down* which involved him taking over an empty shop in Oxford Street, London and publicly destroying everything he owned. He did this by having some sort of conveyor belt feeding all his worldly goods, including a work of art by another name artist, into one of those machines you see council parks and gardens workers feeding with branches and woodchips come flying out the other end. This took no more than a week to do and attracted an audience of over 40,000. It established his reputation and he was able to move on, getting on with the other stuff he was doing. Me, I am still stuck with more than 10,000 bits to go and what now seems to be a bit of a pale and second-hand idea.

Mid 2005 I was longing to be shot of the whole thing. Desperate measures were being called for. The thing at Baltic had worked, so I accepted an offer to do it at the Greenbelt Festival. This is a Christian festival that has been going for over 20 years. I had never heard of it before but they told us that they sell out the 20,000 tickets on offer every time. For the past few years they have been holding it on Cheltenham Racecourse. They wanted me to do *How To Be An Artist* in a tent to about 800 people. I told them that I could hardly be described as a practising Christian. They said it did not matter. Maybe I should give it a go. So I said yes. My thinking was that there would be nobody at this festival I know, so if I fuck up it won't matter. John Wesley, the founder of the Methodists, used to preach to open-air congregations of thousands, 250 years ago, with nothing more than his un-amplified voice to put his message over to the crowd. Eight hundred in a tent should be easy-peasy.

John Hirst, Gimpo and myself cut up a 1000 fractions of the Richard Long and stuck them on signed warranty cards in the week leading up to Greenbelt. This meant the whole selling process could be streamlined.

It turned out that my performance was not to happen in a marquee but in a huge conference hall. Gimpo insisted that I mic myself up with one of those collar mics that they use for TV interviews. I insisted the mic not be turned on. The place was fair packed out when I strode out from the dressing room. 'Good afternoon, my name is Bill Drummond. I'm here to…' and for the first ten minutes or so I did my best to project my voice and self over to every one of the 800 or so punters in the room without the help of amplification. That was up until a large section of the audience towards the back started to shout something at me.

'We can't hear you.' Them.

'What you saying?' Me.

'We can not hear you.' Them.

'Ya what?' Me.

'WE CANNOT HEAR YOU.' Them.

So I failed where John Wesley had succeeded. The collar microphone got switched on and I was off. And it was a great success, I went down a storm and we sold the 1000 fractions.

I allowed this success to go to my head. I thought maybe I should book the Royal Albert Hall. It holds just over 6000 people. Promote the arse out of the event. Tell the packed audience the doors were locked and none of us were leaving the building until every one of the bits of *A Smell Of Sulphur In The Wind* had been sold. And when the last one had been sold I would walk out of the Albert Hall, get the tube to Heathrow, take the next plane to Iceland and finish the job. But then it was pointed out to me by people I trust that the reality was that I would probably sell 800 tickets and the whole thing would be a massive disaster and at best a damp squib. And that would be that. There would be nowhere else to go literally and metaphorically to get the job done.

So, no Royal Albert Hall. I have resigned myself to the fact that I will carry on doing this forever. It will evolve. It will change. There will be bursts. There will be troughs. There will be days when I want to dump the whole lot in the Grand Union Canal. And on one glorious but probably still far-off day, I will have sold my last slither of the thing and I can head off to Iceland and crawl across it.

After I do a performance, when people are queuing up for me to cut one of the bits out for them, there is always someone who asks a variant of this question:

'Does Richard Long know what you are doing?'

I always answer along these lines:

When I was down at the Arnolfini in Bristol, I was in the gallery space in the afternoon, sitting by the table that had the box that contained *A Smell Of Sulphur…* on it, when in came a couple. The man was tall and in his late 50s, the woman younger with blond hair. The man was wearing a T-shirt with a Richard Long text work on it, one of his Zen-like ones. He had a glance around the space then headed over to me.

'Are you Bill Drummond?'

'Yes.'

'Can you tell me what is going on?'

And I started to give a précised version of the whole thing. The two-minute version. By this time he was joined by his partner. He turned to her and said, 'I may as well buy a bit of it back.'

I then went through the whole thing of him handing over 75p to John Hirst; getting a dollar note back; handing the $1 over to me; doing the lottery thing with the DOWN bag and the ACROSS bag; finding the co-ordinates on *A Smell of Sulphur...* It turned out to be one of the white bits. The man wearing the Richard Long T-shirt wanted to know why I was selling off bits of the mounting card. I took some small delight in explaining that according to the artist, Richard Long, the whole thing was the work of art. I lifted the frame up and showed him the label on the back where it stated that the artwork measured 1.12m x .81m. He accepted this. I stuck his fraction on a warranty card, signed it as the seller, and asked him to sign it as the buyer. He did. I then asked him to do his bit on the SOLD painting and lastly put his name, the co-ordinates of the fraction that he had purchased, the date and his email address into the log book we keep.

'I do not have an email address.'

'Never mind, just put your name and the other stuff.'

He did.

He then turned to his partner and said, 'A gift for my solicitor.'

And left the gallery. His partner stayed for a bit longer taking in some of the stuff on the walls.

A couple of minutes later Julian, the bloke from the Arnolfini bookshop, came running in.

'Sorry about that, Bill. There was no way we could warn you and he has tickets for tonight's performance.'

In all the time I had been a fan of the work of Richard Long I had never seen a photo of him, had no idea what he looked like. Had no interest in him as a person.

Later, sitting in the storeroom that doubled as my dressingroom, I once again contemplated doing a runner. The knowledge that Richard Long was sitting out there in the audience was almost too much for me to bear. The storeroom did not have a window. The only way out was through the gallery and past the expectant audience. There was nothing for it. I did the only thing I could do — I made my entrance.

'Good evening, my name is Bill Drummond...'

And I spent the next hour and a half doing my routine with the man with the Richard Long T-shirt sitting in the front row, not more than 9 feet away from me.

After my performance and the queue of people wanting to buy bits of *A Smell of Sulphur...* formed, the man with the T-shirt stayed sitting in his chair. The queue took the best part of an hour to dwindle to a couple of stragglers. That man kept sitting there. The last customer left, the man stood up, lifted his chair, placed it beside me, sat down and said, 'I think we have some things to discuss, Bill.' And we spent the next 30-odd minutes discussing. He wanted to know why I had so many chips on my shoulder about the art world. He wanted to know why I had chosen him to have a go at the art world. He wanted to know why I felt the need to make work that piggy-backed on other artists' endeavours to get noticed, this was in reference to the K Foundation Award/Turner Prize/Rachel Whiteread thing back in 1993, as well as his own work. He also wanted to know what Tammy Wynette was like.

As to what he thinks of what I have done or do, I still have no real idea. I hope he thinks there is more to it than he thought before he came to that evening's performance. Of course I wish I had not met him. I hope it will not taint my appreciation of the work he has done. For me his work is still the visual art that has most inspired and invigorated me over the last 25 years. And, yes, I cannot deny that the sheer scale and bloody-minded effort that goes into doing what he does fills me with awe and respect. It is in acknowledgment of this that makes his parting remark to me seem strange, but in some way inspiring and reassuring.

'It is easier the way I do it, Bill.'

In the prologue and at the beginning of the epilogue to this book, I mentioned how I no longer lived in the same house. One of the stated aims of this whole thing was to replace the original *A Smell Of Sulphur In The Wind* with *A Smell Of Money Underground* on my bedroom wall, so I could have a daily relationship with the work that could rival and compliment the view across the Vale of Aylesbury from my then bedroom window.

It has been suggested by a colleague that I should ask the new owners, of my old house, if I could come around to their place, hang *A Smell Of Money Underground* on my old bedroom wall, take a photo of it hanging there, then take it down, thank them and leave.

I may or may not do this but more important to me is the space on the wall of my new bedroom that is reserved to hang it. This space is the whole of the wall at the opposite side of the room to where my head lays on the pillow. Right now the first thing that I see when I wake up in the morning is this empty space (or that is the theory). One day this empty wall will have *A Smell Of Money Underground* on it. Until then, the empty space, and after then the work will act as a constant reminder to myself to give a little thought to consequences before acting on any new whim. I will also balance this in my head with the certain knowledge that if whims were not embarked upon, very little of substance in the affairs of man, big and small, would ever be done.

The Epilogue to The Epilogue

21 November 2009

So that was the epilogue written in June 2006. More than three and a half years have slipped by since then. 'So why the hold up?' you may ask yourself. Well, it's because I've put almost all other work on hold to concentrate on The17. I have given myself until 28 April 2013 to get The17 done, and only then will I return to completing this job. That's if nothing untoward happens in the meantime. 'So why publish this now?' I allowed myself to get talked into it, I mean the words were just lying in my drawer anyway, and I loved the idea of the cover and title and wanted the buzz of walking into a bookshop and seeing it there.

Also I should add that I am writing this *Epilogue to The Epilogue* on the 21 November 2009 while in Linz, Austria. Today is No Music Day; since writing the bit about No Music Day in the epilogue proper, I made the decision to limit my direct involvement with No Music Day to five years. Today is the final No Music Day of the five-year plan. And today I have allowed myself to go through the whole lot and write this bit at the end of it all.

Editorial consultation: Rosa Ainley, Chris Brook & John Hirst.
Design and art direction by Cally at www.antar.cc.
PR by Maija Handover at Sound UK
Published by Beautiful Books in association with The Penkiln Burn.